BFI Modern Classics

Rob White
Series Editor

BFI Modern Classics is a series of critical studies of films produced over the last three decades. An array of writers explore their chosen films, offering a range of perspectives on the dominant art and entertainment medium in contemporary culture. The series gathers together snapshots of our passion for and understanding of recent movies.

Do the Right Thing

Ed Guerrero

 Publishing

3-26-2003
WW
#12.95

First published in 2001 by the
British Film Institute
21 Stephen Street, London W1T 1LN

The British Film Institute promotes greater
understanding and appreciation of,
and access to, film and moving image
culture in the UK.

British Library Cataloguing-in-Publication Data
A catalogue record for this book is available
from the British Library

ISBN 0-85170-868-4

Series design by Andrew Barron &
Collis Clements Associates

Typeset in Italian Garamond and Swiss 721BT
by D R Bungay Associates, Burghfield, Berks

Printed in Great Britain by
Norwich Colour Print, Drayton, Norfolk

Contents

TO THE MEMORY OF MY FATHER, 'THE BIG G'

Acknowledgments

Besides the basic research and multiple drafts, good film books are always fed by good company, consisting of exuberant conversation and debate about the movies with colleagues and friends. This has certainly been the case with the production of this monograph, so my thanks go out to all those who have done some basic hanging out with me and shared their opinions about black cinema and its critical discourse. I want to especially thank my colleague Toby Miller for the relevant hook-ups, and much illuminating discussion during the writing of this project.

I also want to thank my colleagues at NYU – Bob Stam, Anna McCarthy, Bob Sklar, Sheril Antonio, Richard Wesley, Mary Schmidt Campbell, Fred Moten, Manthia Diawara and Clyde Taylor. But many thanks also go out to my wife Alvina Quintana, as well as Ella Shohat, Lane Hirabayashi and Marilyn Alquizola, Charlotte and Houston Baker, Herman Gray and Rosa Linda Fregoso, Elaine Kim, Paula Massood, Arlette Frund, Peter Feng, Jesse Rhines, Alessandra Speciale, Lucas Hilderbrand, Carol Henderson, and the late Barbara Christian, good friends, scholars and intellectuals all. They have been great company and provided invaluable insight into the dynamic of black cinema and its attendant politics and culture.

Spike Lee, director, on set

Do the Right Thing

No doubt this film is gonna get more heat than any other film I've done. I know there will be an uproar about this one. ... We're talking white people and racism in a major motion picture. It will be interesting to see how studios deal with it. This film must have a wide, wide release. I have to have major assurances going in.

Spike Lee[1]

1

As he suggests in this opening inscription, Spike Lee draws upon a number of skills as writer, producer, director and marketeer to push his films to popular success. But perhaps more than anything else among his many talents and attributes, Lee is an issues-oriented film-maker whose work is always, in some way, grounded in collective, social values. Indeed, the controversies and representational politics of urban *blackness* are his fortune. All of Lee's films radically and thematically depart from one another, each marking a break with the style and content of its predecessor, with each film situated in its particular historical moment, attendant set of issues and circumstances of production, with none adhering to a particular formula or genre. Significantly, each of Lee's films is organised around a social issue, political conflict, or a personal theme, mixed with an insightful rendering of the subtle nuances and rhythms of African American culture and urban life. Additionally, while the Lee strategy of portraying the dramatic tensions built around an array of conflicts with personal and social consequences is hardly new to the film industry, Lee has been quite adept and successful at feeding off the media attention generated by the controversies surrounding many of his productions. Not incidentally, this high media visibility has greatly contributed to Lee's star persona and public caché as one of America's most recognisable and prolific film makers, and even the most cursory examination of these debates and polemics is revealing.

The controversy over *School Daze* (1988) erupted when Lee's satirically frank depiction of the colour and caste contradictions of black collegiate life (the Wanabees vs. the Jigaboos) didn't agree with the conservative 'uplift the race' vision of the administration of Moorhouse College. Consequently, Lee, a third-generation Moorhouse man, was denied use of the college as a location in mid-shooting schedule. With *Mo' Better Blues* (1990) came accusations of anti-semitism, prompting Lee to rebut these claims in the public forum of *The New York Times*.[2] The release of *Jungle Fever* (1991) raised criticism that Spike Lee's personally narrow views on interracial romance had doomed *Jungle Fever*'s adventurous 'mixed' couple, while simultaneously fetishising and selling the allure of interracial sex and contrasting skin colours.[3] Besides running over studio-imposed budget limits and confronting an array of money issues, the filming of *Malcolm X* (1992) was further complicated by public debates with a number of black critics (Amiri Baraka and bell hooks notable among them) over just who has the 'cultural authority' to film Malcolm's life, and from what historic, social, political, or gendered

Malcolm X

Summer of Sam

perspective.[4] In fact, film industry, media and critical strife generated by the production of *Malcolm X* became so intense that Lee was inspired to inscribe the film's accompanying production book, *By Any Means Necessary: The Trial and Tribulations of the Making of Malcolm X*, with the insurgent subtitle 'with fifty million motherfuckers fucking with you'.[5] Closing the decade, *Summer of Sam* (1999) provoked the ire of some Italian Americans and again raised the perennial 'cultural authority' debate over just who has licence to represent a given social collectivity or identity. *Bamboozled* (2000) further challenged and complicated issues and debates concerning the cinematic construction of *blackness* by painfully (and playfully) exploring the resurrection of the 'coon' stereotype and minstrelsy in the media. Broadly then, Spike Lee's features reveal a restless, developmental experimentation and creativity over what is an ongoing, successful and fast-moving trajectory of issues-focused films made increasingly popular by media-hyped public debate and controversy.[6]

As Lee refuses to dwell long on any specific genre, formula or style, a few constants feed his vision and sustain his work: his commitment to depicting an intimate, nuanced view of contemporary African American culture; his engagement with hotly contested issues of politics, social power, and identity; his persistence at maintaining his momentum over a series of films as he says 'like the white boys do'; and his insistence on not being 'chumped off' by the film industry, but on 'getting paid.'[7]

2

Released 30 June 1989 and falling between the grandly ambitious but somewhat uneven comedy-musical *School Daze* and Lee's exploration of jazz, romance and patriarchy *Mo' Better Blues*, *Do the Right Thing* was much anticipated, widely praised, denounced and debated, clearly drawing more media attention than any other film that summer season of commercial releases. In terms of engaging the politics of race, representation, cultural difference and power, *Do the Right Thing* couldn't have arrived at a more turbulent and opportune, media-focused moment locally, nationally, internationally. Locally, New York City had already been rocked by a series of racially charged incidents including the dramatic and questioned Twana Brawley rape case, the violent and sensationalised rape of a white jogger in Central Park by a group of black youths, as well as a long ongoing series of starkly racist, mob killings of African Americans, notably including Michael Griffiths and Yusuf Hawkins whose names were invoked in the film's opening. Adding to the city's tense mix of race, identity and politics, Lee openly remarked on several occasions that he

The release poster

Political graffiti

hoped *Do the Right Thing* would sway the upcoming mayoral election by convincing black voters to unseat then-mayor, Ed Koch, whom he blamed for New York's poisoned racial climate. In one of Lee's many visual details and astute touches that centres the film in the controversies and political contests of the day, the public address of *Do the Right Thing*'s wall graffiti plays with the slippery, contingent qualities of mass mediated truth. Lee proclaims with situational irony, on one wall, that 'Twana told the truth', while declaring with literal intent that the voting public should get out the vote and 'dump Koch' on another.

The charged, political, critical and media atmosphere at *Do the Right Thing*'s moment of release was, also, partly energised by sharply exploding controversies in the realms of American art and cultural production, as the nation's political right wing (coincident with a worldwide upsurge of religious fundamentalism) became politically visible and increasingly vocal about policing issues of 'decency' in the arts, humanities, and popular forms of cultural production and consumption. With the slow disintegration of the Soviet Union and its alliances, and the fall of the Berlin Wall marking the official end of the Cold War, the United States was left with no grand ideological scheme or external counter-point,

superpower enemy, to define, unify and defend its citizenry against. Thus the complex weave of political debates and tensions between America's Left and Right, rich and poor, white and non-white, straight and gay, tended to sharpen and implode, focusing on escalating struggles over religion, culture, class and an array of identity and group differences.

The specifics of this debate erupted into open strife in the US Congress as legislators fought over the use of public money for what the political and religious Right deemed as 'indecent' controversial art, principally funded through the National Endowment of the Arts and the National Endowment of the Humanities. From a Congressional uproar over public funding for Andres Serrano's sculpture *Piss Christ* (a crucifix suspended in a bottle of urine), to public outcry and political pressure forcing the cancellation of *The Perfect Moment* exhibition, containing Robert Mapplethorpe's controversial homoerotic photos at Washington DC's prestigious Cochran Gallery, battles over taxpayer funding of the arts raged in both national legislative houses. This battle also rippled through the commercial sector, from Pepsi Cola's dropping Madonna from a lucrative endorsement contract over the potent mix of erotic fantasy with religious ecstacy in her music video 'Like a Prayer' to Martin Scorsese's unflattering, to some blasphemous, rendering of Jesus in his film *The Last Temptation of Christ* (1988). And on the international front, Iranian clerics issued a death sentence, or *fatwa*, against renowned author Salman Rushdie for his novel *The Satanic Verses* which they deemed an insult to Islam.

Across a broad contested terrain, then, the end of the 80s brought America's right wing discourse on 'traditional family values' tagged the 'culture wars', aimed at policing the moral content of public art and culture to its highest point of expression and controversy. This high moment of the 'culture wars' also had a distinct black dimension to it: some in Congress protested the use of Public Broadcasting System money to fund Marlon Riggs's *Tongues Untied* (1991), a breakthrough, poetic documentary exploring the possibilities of a straight-gay 'brother to brother' dialogue, with open proclamations of homoerotic love between black men. Consonant with the same tone of backlash, Langston Hughes's estate supported by a faction of irate, conservative black literati attempted to block the US screening of Isaac Julien's short feature *Looking for Langston* (1988), a dreamy, erotic meditation set in the Harlem Renaissance and celebrating Hughes's clandestine homosexuality. The end of the 80s also saw an unlikely alliance between some African American civic and church leaders, and America's white neo-conservatives aimed at proscribing the lyrics and attitudes of young black hip-hop and rap performers. So it was in this time frame and charged atmosphere of political and cultural conflict that *Do the Right Thing* came to spark more media attention and critical debate than any other film in the history of black American film-making (with *Sweet Sweetback's Baadasssss Song* [1971] perhaps taking a worthy second place).

Always pushing *Do the Right Thing*'s promotion and his public persona as director, actor, celebrity, that summer Spike Lee loomed large in the media, appearing on the covers of three national magazines including *Newsweek* and *The Nation*. But perhaps Lee appeared most tellingly on the cover of *American Film*, where, signalling his commitment to desegregating yet another American enterprise, he posed in a Dodgers' uniform (Jackie Robinson's, no less) leaning forward and set to pitch a wicked, social curve-ball, and in an act of symbolic conflation moved the contested terrain of racial exclusion from baseball of the past, to the 'now' of the commercial film industry. Moreover, *Do the Right Thing*'s social and political influence was deemed important enough to impel both *The Oprah Winfrey Show* and *Nightline* to devote entire programmes to the film's broad reception and social impact. *The New York Times* ran at least five articles, a symposium of critics and experts on cinema, violence and race, a couple of Sunday features, as well as several reviews of the film. As noted by the flood of reviews, Spike Lee interviews, cameos, bios, photo opps, and various articles weighing the impact of the film's social, political and aesthetic representations, all the major papers in the country debated *Do the Right Thing*, taking positions somewhere between, or at, one of the extreme poles of opinion – with the film deemed socially diagnostic and prescient, at one end, or a dangerous cinematic provocation to violence at the other. Likewise, the *Village Voice* ran eight substantial articles on *Do the Right Thing*, with one notably contentious 'Negro' critic provocatively deploying Susan Sontag's critique of Hitler's favourite film maker, Leni Riefenstahl, to accuse Spike Lee of an 'Afro-Fascist chic' based on a 'reemergence of black power thinking', and a 'bootlegged '60s' perspective on race and racism. Stanley Crouch pressed his vitriolic and personal attack by comparing *Do the Right Thing* to a 'turd' pushed into white liberal faces. He concludes his assault by likening Lee to executed mass murderer 'John Wane Gacey in a clown suit'.[8]

Yet another notable local polemic, making the most automatic, conservative establishment charge against *Do the Right Thing* was penned

by Joe Klein in *New York* magazine. In his June 1989 article Klein deploys a traditional tactic used by the commercial film industry to deal with feature films that are set beyond or violate the ideological limits of scripts, narratives, representations and agendas that uphold Hollywood's interpretation of the dominant social norm. When a commercial film depicting a social issue or perspective challenges Hollywood's strategies of ideological containment, that film usually comes under attack for inflaming and exacerbating the very

Jack Johnson, Heavyweight champion

problem that it seeks to expose, engage or change. One of the most common forms of this manoeuvre is to claim that social critique or challenge to the status quo automatically incites reactionary mob violence. This move is as old as commercial film-making itself and finds its origins in early media racism and censorship, with perhaps the most famous example (of many) being the first black World Heavyweight Boxing Champion Jack Johnson's stunning defeat of the 'Great White Hope' and virulent racist, Jim Jeffries. The budding, and already white-dominated, film industry hoped to make enormous profits from what would be the biggest fight film ever by filling the cinemas with white men wishing to underscore their supremacy and restore a threatened sense of masculinity by enjoying the spectacle of Gentleman Jim Jeffries thrashing the black champion and taking back the title. But on that 4 July 1910, it was Jeffries who took the thrashing. Consequently, all Jack Johnson boxing films – and eventually all boxing films – were banned on the thin pretext that their exhibition would incite violence.[9] Since then, this strategy has been reflexively played to many variations in movie history, from claims that *The Man With the Golden Arm* (1955) would encourage illicit drug use, to blaming the classic American gangster genre (such as *The Public Enemy* [1931]) and contemporary 'hood-homeboy-action' flicks like *New Jack City* (1991) and

The Man With the Golden Arm

The Public Enemy

Menace II Society (1993) for encouraging and glamorising violence and the criminal life.

Accordingly, Joe Klein makes the most common conservative objection against *Do the Right Thing*: that ultimately, the film is an incitement to racial violence. Sounding the alarm to circle the wagons against an impending black uprising, Klein inverts and projects his own fear and malevolence towards young black men, masking his hostility with the thin rhetoric of self-defence. He accuses *Do the Right Thing* of implicitly telling black teenagers that 'the police are your enemy ... Whites are your enemy'. Broadly, when it comes to the social value of black men, they all look alike to Klein. It is guilt by association, as he casts a wide net, essentialising and tainting all black males with the onus of urban crime and violent, antisocial behaviour, regardless of their accomplishments or contributions to society. Klein not so subtly smears David Dinkins's bid for the mayor's office and the future of Spike Lee's film career, with what he quite wishfully speculates will happen if *Do the Right Thing* were to incite violence akin to that of the black youth gang involved in the notorious and brutal Central Park rape and 'wilding' incident. Making the same case in more subdued tones, in his review in the same June 1989, *New York* magazine, David Denby writes that 'the explosion at the end of the movie ... should divide the audience, leaving some moviegoers angry and vengeful, others sorrowful and chastened. ... But if Spike Lee is a commercial opportunist, he's also playing with dynamite in an urban playground. The Response could get away from him.'[10] In the summer of 1989, New York City, along with many other urban combat zones, could not have been more tense and divided along racial lines, and judging from the social and material inequality of their lived relations the social dynamite was already in place – black people hardly needed the pretext of a movie to explode.

So it's not really surprising that Lee, being one of the very few black film-makers to consistently challenge the white hegemony of the commercial film industry on its own turf and terms (raising finances and making one feature film after another and getting paid), is well aware of the general anxiety and resistance aroused in dominant cinema and its attendant cultural apparatus by any African American who dares to project on the big screen his or her unfiltered and often contrary views of American life and racial power relations. Early on in his conceptual musings about the project, Lee notes that while hawking the script around to the studios, Paramount Pictures pulled the plug on negotiations when he refused to soften the film's explosive, frenzied climax. Lee clearly understood the stakes in the game, saying that 'they want an ending that they feel won't incite a giant Black uprising. They are convinced that Black people will come out of the theaters wanting to burn shit down.' Fully comprehending the studio's generalised dread of the socially charged categories of *race* and *difference* he emphatically surmises that his script is 'TOO BLACK AND TOO STRONG'.[11] It was not long before Spike Lee's anticipations about its critical reception were confirmed. For as the scholarly discourse on *Do the Right Thing* has pointed out, with the film's release the white press broadly portrayed Spike Lee as an angry black urban youth. And by stereotyping him thus, the mainstream media were able to distort and overlook *Do the Right Thing*'s complex mediation of racial power relations, while simplistically reducing the film's complex argument to a sensational exploitation of violence.[12] Suffice it to say, events proved the likes of Klein and Denby wrong, as the racial apocalypse forecast by conservatives, some film critics, studios, distributors and cinema owners never materialised. Seemingly, when it comes to *race*, Hollywood's strategies for upholding the perspectives of the dominant social order while containing the challenges of all *others* intensify and operate from deep historical and psychological dimensions of fear and guilt. Thus any film exploring and questioning black–white power relations from a black, counter-current perspective is automatically viewed as a threat by the studios and the establishment media.

Overall, however, the criticism, reviews and general publicity for *Do the Right Thing* tilted in the film's favour by a contentiously thin 'split decision'. Lee noted that the accusations of critics like Klein and Denby hurt the film's crossover potential in the first critical weeks that measure box-office success, in that 'they kept a lot of white moviegoers away from the theaters. They decided that they'd see the film on videotape because they were not going to risk being shot or stabbed by angry mobs of black folks.'[13] Contrarily, the larger point and irony of the media frenzy caused by *Do the Right Thing*, is that all of the controversy and publicity has, largely, worked to Spike Lee's advantage. In spite of his considerable auteur caché and influential celebrity persona, Lee is viewed by Hollywood's executive offices as a marginal small to mid-budget maker of 'niche market' films.[14] This is because Lee has never had the full backing and benefit of the industry's vast promotional publicity machine, which is reserved for mainstream movies and especially its blockbusters.[15] Noting this budgetary marginalisation driven by Hollywood's perception of market, throughout his career, Lee has consistently complained about the industry's tendency to see black people as a 'monolithic audience' at Hollywood's command, a captive social formation of unvarying consumer tastes with no class distinctions or differences in social or regional orientation. Perhaps Lee most sharply articulates his concern about his marginalisation and the games played by the film industry in his comments about the lack of promotional support for his preceding picture, *School Daze*. Lee criticises Columbia Pictures in the frank, black street vernacular that has become his cinematic signature, and that has served him so well in the gritty urban dialogue of some of his best scripts. He writes of the studio that, 'all they see is niggers: nigger director and nigger audience, second-rate, second class shit: therefore the project is not worth their time and money'. Lee goes on to speculate that when he has to promote the film himself to make it a success, the studio 'without any effort on their part, … will claim they knew it all along'.[16]

Consequently for Lee, self-generated promotion and publicity leading to any media attention – good or bad, just not indifferent – has always been recognised by him as a winning gambit: this has contributed to *Do the Right Thing*'s popular exposure, market position and commercial success. However, the ironic upshot to all of *Do the Right Thing*'s successful mega-media attention resulting from Lee's shrewd 'promo and press' campaign aptly bespoke of his ambivalent and outlying position in the dominant industry. For, in spite of all of the film's publicity and Lee's high media profile, *Do the Right Thing* received little recognition at the highest business and institutional levels of Hollywood. Contrary to the feelings of many film critics, cineastes and fans that the film should have won the award for Best Picture, and Spike Lee the award for Best Director, the 1990 Academy Awards Ceremony granted *Do the Right Thing* two scant nominations, for Best Writing and Best Supporting Actor. The Academy Awards all but ignored the film during its TV gala, sending it home with an Oscar for Best Writing, Screenplay Written Directly for the Screen, a relatively minor category. The snub is hardly surprising when one considers Hollywood's stunted policies pertaining to non-white *difference* and representational power relations with the dominant white norm. Evincing its policies the 1989 Oscar for Best Picture went to *Driving Miss*

Driving Miss Daisy

Dances With Wolves

Daisy, and in 1990 it went to *Dances With Wolves*, the two hit, mainstream features that aptly sum up the scope of the Hollywood calculated and stagnant liberalism when dealing with race on the big screen: a narrow range of clichés, from the paternalist problem picture with its long-suffering black servant, to the revisionist Western with the Indians, now the good guys, in an alliance with updated 'gone native', eco-friendly whites. The contrasts between Morgan Freeman's rendering of an elderly, humble and enduring Negro servant in *Driving Miss Daisy*, and Spike Lee's insurgent portrayal of the feckless, defiant urban youth Mookie could not have been greater in the 1989 Oscar year. For Hollywood however, the issue was simple: to make money for the industry at the box office in a 'niche market' category, partly dependent on crossover receipts was one thing, to be awarded the highest level of white establishment recognition and acclaim (whether deserving or not) was quite another.

Yet the travesty of *Do the Right Thing*'s neglect by the film industry that year, reveals an important money dimension related to the way the movie business manipulates the financing, production and promotion of what it considers 'black films'. At this writing, for a 'white' mainstream feature film to be regarded a success it has to earn at least three and a half times its production budget at the box office. Black films, because of their popular cultural themes and styles, their concentrated, guaranteed black audience combined with the bonus of a broader crossover youth audience, and because the industry invests so little money in them compared to mainstream productions, consistently come in above the standard 3.5:1, box office profit-to-production cost ratio. In short, black films are cheap to produce and, importantly, almost always make money. But this also means that black films are unfairly held to a double standard. In order to be deemed successes in industry terms, they have to earn more money on drastically smaller production and promotion budgets than mainstream, big-budget blockbuster productions. So, even though it was profitable and popular, earning a healthy $27.5 million on production costs of $6.5 million, well above the 3.5:1 industry standard, and reaching a respectable 45th position out of a listing of 124 titles in *Variety*'s end-of-the-year 'Big Rental Films of 1989 …',[17] *Do the Right Thing* would have to win industry and institutional acceptance the way other films regarded as outsider, art-house, or in this case 'black' productions have had to: over time, with institutional hindsight and cumulative critical recognition as a unique masterwork – that is, in dominant cinema terms, as a 'classic'. In this regard, *Do the Right Thing* and Lee decisively measure up to the standard put forth by critic and scholar Leo Braudy when he observes that 'the film "classic" creates its own special audience through the unique power of the film making artist's personal creative sensibility'.[18] I would add that the

Spike Lee celebrity persona, combined with the timing and relevance to the political and social debates of *Do the Right Thing*'s ongoing, historical moment have had much to do with the film's elevation to 'classic' status.

Further underscoring Hollywood's schizophrenia, by which a film can be an influential money-maker and social marker, and yet marginal to the industry's business and ideological agendas, many established film critics disagreed with the verdict of the industry-dominated Academy Awards Ceremony, and in their own organisations recognised *Do the Right Thing*'s aesthetic and political significance as well as its broad popularity. Gene Siskel of the *Chicago Tribune* praised the film as being as good as *The Godfather* calling it 'one terrific movie'. Noting Spike Lee's creativity on multiple levels of production and promotion, Vincent Canby of *The New York Times* remarked that Lee was 'the most distinctive American multi-threat man since Woody Allen'.[19] Suitably, *Do the Right Thing* won in 1989 at both the Los Angeles Film Critics' Association Awards for Best Picture, and at the New York Film Critics' Circle Awards, which gave Best Cinematography to Ernest R. Dickerson. Also that year the film was nominated for the Golden Palm at Cannes. Over time, and due to the social relevance and persistence of its many issues, an ever-expanding volume of critical and academic writing on the film, as well as its continued audience and critical recognition as an outstanding, contemporary classic, *Do the Right Thing* has proved its creative stamina and ongoing import to current social concerns. Ten years after its release, in the first year that it was eligible for nomination, 1999, the Library of Congress' National Film Preservation Board honoured *Do the Right Thing*, declaring it a national treasure and putting it on its prestigious list for preservation, the National Film Registry.

3

Do the Right Thing's story-line is direct and simple enough. An ensemble of neighbourhood characters, concentrated on a single city block, play out the tensions of the hottest day of a Brooklyn 'Bed Sty' summer. Tensions build, until a series of small aggravations ultimately culminate in a racialised explosion of multicultural dimensions and disastrous consequences. However, this straight trajectory to riot and mayhem tends to belie the complex, tangled web of power relations, representations, personal and social interactions and negotiations that make the film's discourse so powerfully edgy, tragicomic and relevant to the issues the film explores and that are still very much with us. In weaving this complex, underpinning political and social discourse, as well as the collective explosion that culminate in the film's dénouement, Lee had much in the daily experience of black New Yorkers to draw upon, from police brutality, racial profiling, neighbourhood colonisation and gentrification, to gender and family relations and the tensions of identity politics, to non-white immigration, and the persistent travails of systemic racism.

As Lee notes in his journal, the initial inspiration for the film was the 1986 Howard Beach incident, in which a black man, Michael Griffiths, was chased down and murdered by a gang of white youths for the egregious offence of asking for directions at a 'white' pizza parlour. But Lee mentions more names: Eleanor Bumpers, Yusuf Hawkins, Michael Stewart. Unfortunately, the list is long, for these occurrences, issues and injustices are permanent and ongoing, surfacing in our electronic and print media with a depressing regularity. Thus *Do the Right Thing* interrogates the superficially congenial, but often deeply strained, interactions between a range of characters, a multicultural mix of races, ethnicities and social alignments brought together for varied purposes on the block, the contested cultural turf of a predominantly African American and Puerto Rican, working-to-lower-class neighbourhood.

If Spike Lee is mainly viewed as the maker of modest films with an art-house bent, then small to mid-budget productions with an ensemble cast (examples being *She's Gotta Have It* [1986], *Jungle Fever*, *Get on the Bus* [1996], *Girl 6* [1996] and *Bamboozled*), have been Lee's most

effective stratagem to gain the creative freedom of control over the script, along with the 'get paid' rewards of popular circulation and financial success. While by no means satisfied with the Hollywood-imposed budget ceiling on black film-makers, Lee has understood how to maximise his position well, arguing that he has had to trade larger budgets for 'full creative control' of his projects. So for many reasons *Do the Right Thing* stands out – its controversy, its popularity and its acclaim.

The narrative's long and fateful twenty-four hours opens with a wake-up call delivered by the community's store-front radio disc jockey Mister Senor Love Daddy (Sam Jackson). It is a thematic refrain in Lee's films – a call linked to, and evoking the last resolving cry of *School Daze* – and it is echoed again at the end of *Jungle Fever*. Thus it carries the literal meaning of waking up to the possibilities and opportunities of the day, but also figuratively waking up to higher levels of social realisation and personal consciousness. As Lee's assembly of characters stir from sweaty, uncomfortable sleep to the radio's wake-up call to assume their individual roles and social functions on the block, we are nonchalantly introduced to their subjectivities and roles in the larger story world. A gritty and grey old man, Da Mayor (Ossie Davis), the block's resident alcoholic and sage, stirs and comments on the heat. After a moment we see Mookie (Spike Lee) awake in his sister's apartment, engaged in a definitive act of characterisation, carefully and obsessively counting his saved up money. Mookie then goes into his sister Jade's (Joie Lee) bedroom

Nola Darling in *She's Gotta Have It*

to playfully wake her up. Next, a 1975 El Dorado pulls up in front of 'Sal's Famous Pizzeria' as the owner Sal (Danny Aiello) and his two sons, the virulent tribal bigot Pino (John Turturro) and the timid but fair-minded Vito (Richard Edson) argue and prepare to open the pizzeria to the business of a scorching day. We cut to Mother Sister (Ruby Dee), the block's unofficial matriarch and watch captain, as she leans out her window and converses on the porch with Mookie about the prospects of the approaching hot day.

'Wake up!'

As day progresses more characters show up on the scene. Buggin Out (Giancarlo Esposito), the neighbourhood's self-appointed politico who espouses a passé brand of militant cultural nationalism that finds little support among the block's residents, makes a contentious appearance. His main running buddy and disciple Radio Raheem (Bill Nunn) comes on the scene, a big silent youth whose entire persona and mode of expression come through a huge 'boom box' powered by twenty 'D' batteries, volume pumped up and obsessively playing the film's theme song, Public Enemy's 'Fight the Power'. Then there is Smiley (Roger Guenveur Smith). Disabled and stuttering, Smiley patrols the block advertising the inherent unity of black political aspirations by selling a postcard depicting Malcolm X and Dr Martin Luther King smiling and shaking hands. Permanently installed on the end of the block and functioning as an Afro-Greek chorus, punctuating the day's narrative with their wry commentary, are the idle 'corner men' – Sweet Dick Willie (the late Robin Harris), ML (Paul Benjamin) and Coconut Sid (Frankie Faison). Also jobless and basically just hanging out for the summer, we see a cohort of black teens – Cee (Martin Lawrence), Punchy (Leonard Thomas), Ella (Christa Rivers), and Ahmad (Steve White). In addition, we

Trio

are introduced to the Puerto Rican mother of Mookie's infant son, Tina (Rosie Perez), who throughout the narrative is constantly on Mookie's case about being a more emotionally involved partner and productive, responsible father.

It is also Tina who first signals the complex, layered tensions and ambiguities that pervade the film, and more broadly, Lee's art. At the film's first credit roll, the 'Forty Acres and a Mule' production logo appears, accompanied by the sound of an alto saxophone playing a solitary refrain from the 'Negro national anthem' 'Lift Every Voice and Sing'. The scene and music then suddenly cut to Tina doing what Lee tags a 'vicious' hip-hop dance number combining a tense energetic feminine eros and masculine pugnacity as the opening titles and credits come up. Against a staged backdrop of blown-up photos depicting the Bed Sty neighbourhood tinted in the hot sultry, reds, browns and yellows that are ambient throughout the film, Tina deftly gyrates in various skin-tight outfits, shaking and grinding to the pulsing beat, pushing her attractive athletic body through an inventory of hip-hop and boxing moves and metaphors. Tina suggestively bumps and bounces in tights and a short skirt, then in dance skins. Then she deftly shadow boxes to the beat,

Teen quartet

'Fight the Power'

Urban survivalist
slackers

hooking and jabbing in boxing gloves and the silk shorts of a top-rank
contender. The scene is filled in with the boom box proclamations of
'Fight the Power', as the rap group Public Enemy declares 'Elvis was a
racist tried and true. Motherfuck him and John Wayne too!' At the onset
then, we're ready for combat as the political and aesthetic gauntlet is
immediately thrown down. This is straight up cultural war voiced in the
raw street vernacular of today's urban black, hip-hop youth.

In addition, the sonic and ideological leap in this opening credit
sequence – from the race-building criteria of 'Lift Every Voice ...' from
the Negro past, to the contemporary 'keeping it real' protests of 'Fight the
Power' – tells us much about Lee's representational strategies. For while
Spike Lee is a self-proclaimed product of the black college movement, a
Moorhouse man, and while his lineage is definitely grounded in the
middle class 'racial uplift' consciousness and politics of the past, his art
resides in the jolting, unapologetic 'here and now' of today's black urban

youth. As critic Thomas Doherty points out, one of the things that makes *Do the Right Thing* so potent and disturbing to the dominant social norm and Hollywood strategies of racial containment is that the film addresses racism and race relations *today* and solidly in the domestic urban context.[20] Contrary to Hollywood's timid, rear guard approach to racial matters, *Do the Right Thing* does not try to cinematically salve the wounds of the nation's, and particularly the South's, murderous *apartheid* past in the style of *Mississippi Burning* (1988), *Long Walk Home* (1990) or *Ghosts of Mississippi* (1996), nor does it try to displace the onus of racism into another national arena – South Africa, for example, in *A Dry White Season* (1989), or even *Lethal Weapon II* (1989), where the racist villains are white South Africans fighting the bi-racial buddy team of cops played by Danny Gloover and Mel Gibson. Furthermore, Lee refuses to make easy concessions to older 'talented tenth' or 'New Negro' racial improvement, proclamations so famously articulated in the debates and literature of the Harlem Renaissance[21] but still resonant today in overly simplistic calls for 'positive images' of blacks to compensate for the ongoing misrepresentation and slander of African Americans on Hollywood's big screen.

Just as Tina's seductive, opening hip-hop number is fraught with an ambivalent uneasy mix of feminine seduction and masculine threat, so too are *Do the Right Thing*'s characters and narrative disturbingly complex, ambiguous and charged with more than a subtle sense of contradiction. Significantly, the film's protagonist Mookie is hardly an uplifting or compensatory 'positive image' character. Indeed, Mookie is a feckless middleman, a slacker, an urban survival capitalist bent on profitably negotiating all of the neighbourhood's varied racial factions and ambushes, while doing just enough in the way of work to get by. Limited by a rudimentary high school education, trapped in a dead-end job as delivery boy at 'Sal's Famous', obsessed with making cash money 'off the books' and dodging his responsibilities as a father to his son and mate to

Tina, Mookie shows very little ambition or vision as he lives day to day in the narrow confines of the neighbourhood. In one of the film's revealing, mimetic gestures, Tina must order pizzas that Mookie must deliver, just to compel him to visit and relate to her, sexually or otherwise. Similarly, *Do the Right Thing*'s political voices, from loudly overt to suggestively subtle, are rendered in less than heroic terms. These are the voices of complicated and flawed characters, usually more irritating and problematic than they are admirable.

Buggin Out, the main proponent of direct militant action, comes across as his label 'Buggin' suggests, as more an out-of-date, frenzied agitator than a black activist struggling nobly to dismantle white supremacy. And while Radio Raheem certainly doesn't deserve to die for playing his radio too loud, throughout the film he has the distinct air of a bully about him. Lee constructs Raheem as big, inarticulate and intimidating. His laconic address as well as the hip-hop anthem 'Fight the Power' blasting from his radio are more sonic tyranny than musical persuasion. And while Smiley's repeated message is pictorially obvious (that Malcolm and Martin differed over tactics but shared the same goals for black people) his delivery of that message is frustratingly garbled and

(above) Radio Raheem; (opposite) Afro-Greek chorus

rendered impotent by his physical disabilities. The corner men add brilliant, sardonic commentary on the neighbourhood scene and its multicultural politics. But with that commentary cast in the bawdy, cursing argot of the street, they sit, unemployed and powerless, as failed counter-examples to the DuBoisian dream of the 'talented tenth' and the redeeming bourgeois 'positive image'. Likewise, Da Mayor is community-minded, philosophical, but outmoded and haplessly drunk. And the black youths, that challenge Da Mayor's cultural authority and treat him with open contempt are themselves loud, callow, perhaps made uneasy by the dim realisation that Da Mayor's obsolescence looms large in their futures. Even, Tina, while attractive and seductive, is herself, loud, brash and hectoring. As some critics have noted, besides Mookie as a focal point, Sal is perhaps the most fully and sympathetically drawn character of Lee's ensemble. Yet, Sal is the congenial and sometimes contentious, but always paternal, head of what amounts to a pizza plantation, a colonial outpost in native territory. Importantly, it is Sal who, ironically or not, after a long day of petty aggravations, finally explodes in a racist rage that touches off the film's violent, catastrophic climax.

This pervading sense of ambiguity is also manifest in *Do the Right Thing*'s narrative structure, in that no particular character, voice or social orientation is supremely privileged or provides, smug, final answers to the contradictions, issues and grievances raised by the film's stream of polyphonic voices. Importantly, all of these voices, agendas and ideologies stand in tense negotiated relation to each other. Writer and critic Robert Stam's insight into this type of 'ethnic dialogism' well describes the ambiguous tone and unsettled tensions of *Do the Right Thing*'s story world. As Stam puts it 'all utterances inescapably take place against the background of the possible responding utterances of other social and ethnic points of view. Ethnicity is relational, an inscription of communicative processes within history, between subjects existing in relations of power.'[22] One of the many telling moments that exemplifies this ambivalent, dialogic layering of contending discourses and signs occurs in a scene when Mookie orders his sister Jade to stay out of 'Sal's Famous' as he castigates her for being too friendly with Sal, whom he openly accuses of trying to seduce her. Or, as Mookie crassly puts it by way of metaphor, 'All Sal wants to do is hide the salami.' But Jade is quick to counter, pointing out to Mookie that he is long on 'big brother' advice and ultimatums, and short on personal example. She makes it clear that Mookie is living in her apartment, and can hardly keep up with his end of the rent. The discussion ends with Jade getting the best of Mookie and finally declaring that she's tired of 'supporting a grown man'. As a retreating concession, Mookie unconvincingly claims that he will soon 'make a move'. Significantly, they argue against the backdrop of a brick wall, spray-painted with a vivid declaration that becomes clear as the camera ends the scene on a slow, expanding pull-back revealing the wall's message: 'Twana Told the Truth.'

But in the dialogic address and style of the film, did she? Perhaps, a cursory reading of this vignette would support Mookie's position: that Sal is on the make, and by juxtaposition, Twana Brawley, who accused the white

law enforcement establishment of kidnap and rape, did tell the truth. However, as Jade makes clear, Mookie has little authority in *Do the Right Thing*'s story world on which to hang his claims, material, moral, ethical, inferred or otherwise. Moreover, Lee constructs Mookie and Pino as subtle mirror reflections on the issue of romance and separatism, thus tying Mookie more closely to the attitudes of Pino, the outright racist, than perhaps Mookie would care to admit in the contentious racial politics of the neighbourhood. Tellingly, the argument with Jade is preceded in the pizza parlour by Pino and Mookie, linked by the camera's panning eye-line match, as they share the same suspicious look. Slyly gazing in complicity upon Sal and Jade talking over a meal, they both reveal an identical, visceral fear of miscegenation. Consequently, the spray-painted declaration of 'truth' in the Twana Brawley mystery takes on a distinctly relative, tribal tone and is undermined by the polyphonic layering of competing signs, discourses and subject positions; nor after a series of lawsuits and counter-claims, has the Brawley enigma become any clearer in the public imaginary with the passage of time. A similar moment of clashing words and signs occurs when Buggin Out stands in the street and makes the call for the inclusion of black images on Sal's 'Wall of Fame': he is visually contradicted by a huge billboard

Big Brother advice

depicting an ominous, scowling Mike Tyson looming in the background behind him.[23] Moreover, this sense of ambivalence and contradiction takes a linguistic turn when it becomes clear that Buggin Out's understanding of what constitutes a 'positive' image is rudimentary and ironic, at best, as he emphatically declares to Jade that he wants to see some 'black, motherfuckin' pictures on that wall'.

4

Another way to frame the ambiguities and tensions that suffuse most of Lee's films and characters, and especially *Do the Right Thing*, is to view Lee's work generationally, in the context of the emerging consciousness, language and style of a 'new blackness'[24] coming on the scene at the winding down of the Civil Rights Movement and the militant cultural and Black Power politics that briefly followed. African Americans coming of age from the post-Civil Rights late 70s on found themselves in the paradoxical situation of profiting from the institutional gains of the preceding black struggle, advantages that mostly benefited the black middle class, like expanded university admissions, greater access to quality housing, mid-level management jobs and political office that resulted from

The politics of representation

the nation's uneven, grudging efforts at social integration. Yet simultaneously, these 'new blacks' faced a building rearticulation and retrenchment of white conservatism, privilege and outright racism, with all of these ogres subtly coded at the discursive, political and systemic levels. From open claims of black intellectual inferiority in Charles Murray's *The Bell Curve*, to the 'rollback' policies of the Reagan and Bush presidential years (1980–92) aimed at attacking 'affirmative action' programmes and undoing government assistance to black social progress and the social welfare state in general; to the rise of a prison industrial complex leading to an exponentially swelling and disproportionately African American inmate population, white attitudes began to increasingly stiffen against further black and non-white minority progress against the nation's entrenched and systemic racism.[25] By the end of the 80s, the predominant 'backlash' images of the black population were the 'welfare queen', the hood-homeboy gangster and the infamous poster boy of the Bush presidential campaign towards the close of the decade, black criminal Willie Horton.

Post-Civil Rights black identity was further shaped by its own internal currents of consciousness, change and heterogeneity as the ways that one could 'be black' multiplied with increased social integration and various *differences* within the formation of blackness (gay, lesbian, colour, class, gender, bi-racial, disabled etc.) started to emerge. And as forecast in such Blaxploitation flicks as *Superfly,* (1972) and *The Mack* (1973) or the more socially redemptive *Willie Dynamite* (1974), with their narcissistic, coke dealing or pimping heroes, the 70s revealed a distinct shift in black urban youth consciousness and style away from the solidarity of a Black Power 'we' of the 60s, towards a growing individualist, consumer-oriented 'me' generation. Nathan McCall describes this paradigm shift in expressive cultural detail in his autobiographical, black *bildungsroman, Makes Me Wanna Holler*, observing that 'almost overnight, brothers shifted from Black Power chic to gangster buffoon. Suddenly, cats who had been sporting monster Afros broke out the platform shoes, and crushed velvet outfits ...'[26]

Superfly

Sadly, this turn away from collective, political struggle with its demand for social justice and change towards individualism's focus on material self-interest had dire consequences for the communities of black urban America. The advent of improved employment opportunities and more integrated neighbourhoods with better schools allowed the black professional and middle classes to more rapidly move out of inner-city districts, which then became not only race – but now, class-segregated post-industrial ghettoes. Yet, as so vividly depicted in *Do the Right Thing* as well as other films like Darnell Martin's richly detailed *I Like It Like That* (1994), these urban neighbourhoods still retained a strong sense of community and culture. However, they afforded little opportunity or mobility for the lower-class blacks and Latinos left behind and trapped within them. Worse still, blighted with spiraling post-industrial unemployment and crumbling, inferior state schools, these inner city warrens were flooded with crack cocaine, alcohol fortified malt liquor and cheap illegal handguns, all leading to catastrophic results. The violent, socially diagnostic and classic 'hood-homeboy' hits *Boyz N the Hood* (1991) and *Menace II Society* vividly depict the stunted lives, endemic youth violence and soaring homicide rates of the shattered, inner-city terrain. What were once black integral communities were now increasingly becoming fragmented into a dangerous, dystopian landscape spotted with gang hangouts, drug corners and free-fire zones.[27] Or as a cynical white cop in Lee's own discerning exploration of the 'hood-homeboy' turf, *Clockers* (1995), so coldly analogised it, economic and political powerlessness, drugs and homicide had turned what were once thriving communities into 'self-cleaning oven(s)'.

These shifts in the way blacks looked at identity and community were further encouraged by dominant mass media's focusing less on black public and political leadership, and more on the commodification and aggrandisement of blacks as superstar entertainers and sports idols. After a number of disheartening events, like the state's destruction of the Black Panthers in the 70s, or the collapse of the Jesse Jackson-headed Rainbow Coalition following the Democratic National Convention in 1988, a wide range of black hopes for organised, national political power and economic equality were all but snuffed out. In a dubious act of token compensation and strategic co-optation, African Americans began to loom ever larger on the nation's media screens as super-celebrities, super-athletes and super-

Doughboy in *Boyz N the Hood*

criminals. And sometimes these star personae spectacularly covered the full range of media types in a single career trajectory. The cases of O.J. Simpson or Sean 'Puffy' Combs come to mind in this regard. Incidentally, these 'spectacle trials' have turned out to be media bonanzas. In the contest for power as mediated through mass circulated images, African American political and intellectual leadership has been overlooked and displaced by the promotion and symbolic manipulation of popular black icons. And while the proportionally small black middle class has expanded, the great mass of black people have made little, if any, social or material progress since the end of the 60s.[28] All of this 'bad news' is particularly biting and ironic, especially when historian Thomas C. Holt notes that globally 'African-American sports and cultural figures constitute a kind of synecdoche for America'.[29]

Furthermore, the often cited W.E.B. DuBois' concept of the problematic twentieth-century 'color line' has now morphed into a much more layered, multifaceted formulation, perhaps best described as the twenty-first-century problem of the '*difference* line'. Indeed, another consequence of the struggles and gains of the Civil Rights Movement, and the revelation of its strategies combined with the broadly insurgent cultural and political energies of the 60s, was that many other social formations and

movements, such as Chicanos, Asian Americans, Native Americans, feminists, hippies, lesbians, gays and the student New Left forged increasingly organised activist identities that joined in the work of challenging and destabilising the hegemonic power of the dominant white norm. All of these currents of social and cultural change, taken with a swelling influx of non-white immigrants into the USA, which

W.E.B DuBois

started in the 80s, has led to the rise of a multicultural model of race relations that has gradually displaced the traditional binary 'black vs. white' model. Thus the 'new blacks', at least twenty-five years beyond the Civil Rights–Black Power upsurge, increasingly find themselves positioned in a web of shared, overlapping, multifaceted relations with an array of *other* identities, formations and movements striving for recognition, social justice, or merely a fairer and larger piece of the establishment pie.

5

Riding the crest of the 'new black film wave'[30] in his chosen medium and own prolific style, Spike Lee has responded to the complex overdetermining influences – material, cultural and political – that have shaped his generation. He has managed to garner increasingly larger budgets from the Hollywood system, while maintaining all important 'final cut' control over his scripts and avoiding most of the compromises of having to play to a crossover (read white) audience. In a black auteur style reminiscent of pioneering film-makers Oscar Micheaux or Spencer Williams, Lee has managed to make feature films about black life from a black point of view, but with the update that his films cannot be described

Oscar Micheaux

by the limited term 'race movies' as they broadly and popularly circulate through a general audience. Lee has led the wave with cutting edge constructions and articulations of the 'new blackness', and his sustained nuanced revelation of America's 'black urban world'. Thus, Spike Lee ingeniously expounds the complexity of his take on contemporary urban racial politics and culture, as well as the building

tensions that stalk *Do the Right Thing*'s long, hot day in a series of
emblematic vignettes, scenes, and moments. Early on, after Mister Senor
Love Daddy's allegorical wake-up call and announcement of the colour of
the day – black – Lee cuts to a mid-frame, up-angle shot of Smiley in front of
the massive red brick façade of the prosperous, 'Yes Jesus' First Baptist
Church filling the entire frame. Smiley stands bearded, arms outstretched,
apostle-like and simultaneously 'square', in simple clothes (a long-sleeve
shirt buttoned awkwardly at the collar on the hottest day of the year), with an
obsolete piece of consumer junk, a plastic camera/radio combo, slung
around his neck. As he does throughout the film, he holds up a pack of
postcards depicting 'Malcolm and Martin' laughing and shaking hands,
which he points to with a magic marker, as if lecturing or, more appropriately,
preaching the gospel. Here, as Lee does with various characters in numerous
scenes, Smiley's address is more theatrical and staged than the seamless
cinematic 'realism' of Hollywood's classic 'invisible style'. Contrarily, the
scene is a distinct Brechtian moment of 'distanciation' or 'the alienation
effect' by which the work of art simultaneously reveals its own processes of

Preachin' the gospel

production along with society's construction of 'truth'.[31] Smiley speaks directly to the camera and movie audience, so that we momentarily break with the reality of the story world and take special notice of his words. Occurring in front of an established black church, evoking Malcolm and Martin, Smiley's speech conjures up the institutions, leaders, struggles and hopes of the Civil Rights and Black Power past.

But Lee's rendering of this past is itself subtly discanciated and also 'transgressive'.[32] Smiley stammers badly, delivering a frustrated, scrambled, barely intelligible communiqué about Malcolm and Martin, while varying on tactics, standing in unity and agreeing on the necessity to continue the struggle. The scene's political meaning, a tribute to the past and its fallen heroes, while obvious from its visual references, is uncomfortably static, as if the message were eroded over time and beyond the daily concerns of the contemporary black urban scene. Importantly, Smiley's tortured unintelligible soliloquy ends abruptly on the sharply ejected word 'hate', which from this point on, becomes a thematic refrain taken up, discussed, analysed, uttered or performed by several characters during the course of the day. Smiley's scene on the church steps presents us with a noble tale rich in historical insight and sentiment, yet frozen in time, and imperfectly told by the village idiot and/or saint.

So then, one might ask: what of these tensions and issues vexing contemporary black youth and the urban neighbourhood? A revealing moment forecasting the direction of the day's building aggravations, and exhibiting a curious mix of urban youth politics, brand names and street theatre, occurs when a young white urban professional, Clifton (John Savage, who has recently bought a brownstone house on the block), accidentally bumps Buggin Out, scuffing his new sneakers. Furious, and egged on by the block's teen quartet, Buggin Out, true to his name, loudly confronts what the clique perceives as a 'yuppie' interloper, as the scene begins to take on the dramatic trappings of a school-yard fight. Much to the entertainment of a gathering crowd, Buggin demands and gets a weak 'excuse me' from Clifton. But the incident escalates, for this is only entré to an index of underpinning issues and simmering, half-concealed resentments on both sides of the colour/class divide. Inspired by the damage done his new 'Air Jordans' which everyone in the gathering crowd knows cost $100, Buggin derides Clifton for the paucity of his apology and then goes into a poetic litany of issues, criticisms and insults. Bluntly elucidating one of the many social issues nagging the neighbourhood, Buggin finally shouts, 'What do you want to live in a Black neighborhood for? Motherfuck gentrification.' Clifton's answer is equally reflex and one-dimensional, as he responds with the cliché that he is 'under the assumption that this is a free country and one can live where he pleases'.

Of course this assertion hides the skin colour and economic privilege that determine whether Clifton will be able to live, as he says, where he 'pleases'. Clifton's 'free country' argument also carries the assumption that social inequality, now, is a matter of 'choice', and it resonates with the conservative line Sal ends his conversations with when imparting philosophical advice, 'this is America'. Throughout the film the majority of Lee's characters play with the thoughtless, clichéd lines that frame, simplify and distort much of our thinking about race and *difference*. Verbally and visually, the Clifton vs. Buggin Out confrontation is one of the first of a building series over the day – small incidents, with which Lee illustrates the diverse communal battle over stereotypes, group agendas, urban space, language and commodity signs.

In this instance *Do the Right Thing* couldn't have more sharply drawn the political, cultural, material contrasts between the two adversaries, with Buggin Out – black urban youth, living in rented accommodation, dressed in the hip-hop fashion of the day – squared off against white urban professional and property owner, Clifton, in Larry Bird's green, No. 33 Celtics jersey. Clifton is sweaty from exercising but emotionally cool, whereas Buggin Out is visually cool and fashionable with hip-hop haircut and athletic summer court wear, but he is angry and

agitated. By espousing a truncated, hip-hop brand of late 80s cultural nationalism, Buggin Out is clearly not depicted as the admirable champion of a cause or philosophy. Rather, he is a dubious character and regarded with skeptical glances and a chorus of 'hell no(s)' on the block. Buggin Out is a provocateur and agitator, more about the fashions of a 'b-boy', the excitement of bluff and gesture, than deep social commitment or effective social action. While into the drama of confrontation, Buggin Out

(top) Urban collision; (above) 'Motherfuck gentrification!'

is not about to engage in fisticuffs for the entertainment of the local neighbourhood. So he leaves himself a way out, shouting, as Clifton retreats up the steps, that he's just lucky that 'a black man has a loving heart. Next time you see me comin', cross the street quick.' However, issues of race, class and gentrification form only one aspect of this confrontation. In this sense one sees an older politic and set of power relations expressed through various brand names and forms of consumerism, whether bargain-hunting for a brownstone in a deteriorating inner-city neighbourhood, or becoming infuriated over a scuff on your new $100 'Air Jordans'. Yet both Clifton and Buggin Out stake their positions in political rhetoric, Clifton with 'free country' proclamations and Buggin Out with exhortations to neighbourhood youth to 'stay black'. The confrontation ends with Buggin Out shouting for Clifton to 'go back to Massachusetts', and Clifton responding emphatically that he was 'born in Brooklyn'. At this, the crowd, throws up its arms and howls with derision.

And so the long hot day goes, made up of a building series of scenes interrogating various aspects of power, race, racism, gender and the daily negotiations and conflicts of the neighbourhood. Some of these revealing tableauxs, moments, scenes, can be as brief, and yet powerful, as an exchange of passing looks. This is the case when two cops on patrol slowly drive by and trade mutual stares of contempt with the corner men. Residing outside the community, these working-class, white cops only see the surface, the stereotypical threat of idle, black 'suspects'. With mirror looks that defiantly return the gaze, what the corner men see is racist, bullying cops, making their livelihoods as the state army of occupation in a non-white neighbourhood. It's a tense stand-off as both groups come to the same conclusion, muttering the same remark in passing: 'what a waste.' Of course the 'waste' in this fleeting scene is dialogic and multivalent. For it comments on the 'waste' of forced economic idleness, the 'waste' of a smug sense of bigotry, and generally, the social 'waste' of scapegoating and mutual suspicion. In other scenes, the conflict of *differences* is linguistic and always cultural. When Radio Raheem or Da Mayor confront the Korean grocers (Steve Park and Ginny Yang) over batteries or beer, these exchanges are utilitarian and commercial but cast in the raw language and underpinning tensions of the neighbourhood. Not the most well-spoken of characters himself, Radio Raheem ironically harangues the Korean store-keepers about their diction: 'Twenty D batteries, motherfucker. ... Learn English, first.' Again, Lee deploys the mirror effect, by which opposing personalities, ethnicities, social groups, generations tend to mirror each other's perceptions, suspicions and hostilities. Viewed another way, mirroring is the subliminal fear that drives the angry outburst of Ahmad of the teen quartet when he castigates Da Mayor for being a 'drunk zero' undeserving of the respect he gets as a community elder, 'Da Mayor' of the block. Across the generational divide, what Ahmad sees is a little too much of his post-industrial, dead-end future looming in the spectre of Da Mayor, worn out, thrown away and inebriated.

Lee best describes the inner feelings, the fears and alienation of *Do the Right Thing*'s black urban youth ensemble in his production journal when he writes of Mookie and his contemporaries that 'they live for the

'Twenty D batteries'

present moment, because there is nothing they feel they can do about the future. What I'm really talking about is a feeling of helplessness, or powerlessness, that who you are and what effect you can have on things is absolutely nil, zero, jack shit, nada.' By mirroring, Lee extends this ambient feeling of 'jack shit, nada', to Sal's sons, Pino and Vito, for whatever any of the film's characters occupying the mutual turf of the neighbourhood (perhaps excepting Clifton) feel about 'race' they are all

(top) Generations clash; (above) 'jack shit, nada'

mutually trapped by the glass ceiling of class. Thus Lee feeds the subtly escalating tensions of the day.[33]

6

All of these elements – mirroring, mutual suspicion, dialogism, stereotyping, hate speech, scapegoating and explosive anger directed at the racial *other* – come together in the two central, and most commented-upon, scenes of the film: the Mookie/Pino dialogue in the back of the restaurant and the 'racial slur' sequence in the street that follows. After Mookie lays on the phone making small talk to Tina about the subtleties of 'love', Pino loudly complains to Sal that Mookie is causing the pizzeria to lose business. Then as Mookie is about to leave on a delivery, Pino rhetorically asks under his breath, 'how come niggers are so stupid?' To this Mookie angrily rebuts, 'if you see a "nigger", kick his ass'. Vito diplomatically intervenes urging Mookie to 'let it go'. But then the momentum shifts and something subtle and clever happens that deflates the alarmist charge of the critics – David Denby, Joe Klein, Jack Kroll, *et al.* – that *Do the Right Thing* is a reckless incitement to racial violence. Instead of escalating the scene to fisticuffs Mookie takes Pino aside and in a very calm, deliberate manner requests to

Racial dialogue

talk with him for a moment. In the back of 'Sal's Famous', framed in a medium close-up, with the cigarette machine between them as a sort of conference table as they lean on it from opposite sides, Mookie proceeds to very methodically probe and deconstruct Pino's toxic, illogical bigotry. 'Who's your favorite basketball player?' 'Magic Johnson.' 'And not Larry Bird? Who's your favorite movie star?' 'Eddie Murphy.' And so it goes, with all of Pino's favourite athletes, movie and rock stars being black. Mookie springs the trap by pointing out the contradiction and irrationality of Pino's thinking. 'Pino, all you ever talk about is nigger this and nigger that, and all your favorite people are so called niggers.'

Of course Pino doesn't have a coherent answer as he rather ineptly parrots the sentiments of a dominant, post-Civil Rights, white normative culture by which African American celebrities are worshipped as talented and often token 'exceptions', while the great mass of black people are dismissed and marginalised as 'niggers'. According to Pino's thinking 'it's different, Magic, Eddie and Prince are not "niggers", I mean they're not black. Let me explain myself. I mean they're black but not really black. It's different.' Mookie then drops the psychological bomb on Pino, telling him 'You know, deep down inside, I think you wish you were black.' At this, unconsciously underlining the truth of Mookie's observation, Pino bursts out laughing. The scene ends with Pino countering, ridiculing black historical claims and leadership – Jesse Jackson, Al Sharpton and Minister Farrakhan – to which Mookie responds with the fact that black people started civilisation. After more dialogical back and forth, the scene ends in a tacit stalemate and a mutual, almost cordial, exchange of 'fuck you(s)' insulting each group's cultural icons.

Suddenly, we cut to what Lee calls the 'RACIAL SLUR MONTAGE', yet another one of the film's distanciated, cathartic, Brechtian moments, as the heat of the day starts to wear on the character's civility and their social masks start to slip. On the block in the harsh light of this hottest day of the year, a series of working-class men of different races, ethnicities and groups emphatically address the camera and vent their stored anger at a designated racial *other* – Italian Americans, blacks, jews, Koreans, Puerto Ricans. In answer to his dialogue with Pino, Mookie kicks off the montage standing in the middle of the street, framed in a medium shot: 'Dago, wop, garlic-breath, gunia, pizza-slinging, spaghetti-bending, Vic Damone, Perry Como, Luciano Pavarotti, Sole Mio, nonsinging motherfucker.' Cut to the pizza parlour counter and Pino's response: 'You gold-teeth, gold-chain-wearing, fried-chicken-and-biscuit-eatin', monkey, ape baboon, big thigh, fast-running, three-hundred-sixty-degree-basketball-dunking-spade Moulan Yan. Take your fuckin' piece of pizza and go the fuck back to Africa.' Then on the porch, Stevie (Luis Ramos), a Puerto Rican from the neighbourhood: 'You slant-eyed, me-no-speak-American, own every fruit and vegetable stand in New York, Reverend Moon, Summer Olympics '88, Korean kick-boxing bastard' and so on. By cinematically and directly evoking the troubled demons of almost every group's racial id, and letting those demons speak in the raw, unfiltered language of intolerance, prejudice and racism, with this explosive series of rancorous tirades *Do the Right Thing* goes far beyond Hollywood's tame protocol on depicting racial tensions. The harangue builds until community disc jockey Mister Senor Love Daddy finally puts a stop to it, broadcasting over the air one of the few messages unequivocally expressing the film's values: 'yo! Hold up! Time out! Time out! Y'all take a chill. Ya need to cool that shit out … and that's the double truth, Ruth!'

However, beyond Mister Senor Love Daddy's (and the film's) sincere 'double truth' warning, other truths of the montage lurk, ambiguous and complex. Initially, this montage of insults alludes to a similar sequence in Lee's first feature hit, the sexual farce *She's Gotta Have It*, in which a procession of single black men, 'dogs', hilariously deliver their favourite pick-up lines to the camera, such as 'Baby, I'd drink a tub of yo' bath water.' Conversely, in *Do the Right Thing*, the 'slur montage' invokes not cathartic laughter, but a feeling of discomfort

that comes from everyone's uneasy mirror-look at the barely repressed
'devil inside'. The building tension of the racial slur montage also
forecasts the impending social disaster of the film's dénouement. By
pitting various races, identities and groups against each other on the
rawest emotional level, regurgitating their vilest, innermost thoughts and
stereotypes about one another, *Do the Right Thing* depicts the danger
and futility of bigotry and racism at a personal level, from which no

Slur montage: scenes from the racial Id

social formation is exempt. As importantly, this montage works to reveal the *how* of racism while not necessarily addressing racism's greater structural and strategic *why*. That is to say, this litany of racial slurs functions to show how racism works on the interpersonal level, between individuals as targets, representatives of groups, while, perhaps inadvertently, masking the greater why of racism's workings at an institutional, structural level, as a strategy of hidden elites – 'the powers that be' – to keep races, classes and movements divided and fighting among each other, thus distracted from the ignored or concealed, truth of their mutual exploitation. Notably, all of the participants of this montage as working-class males share the same gendered, social orientation. Rather than following *Do the Right Thing*'s, thematic hip-hop call to 'fight the power', these angry, isolated figures representing different races scapegoat and fight each other instead.[34]

In miscellaneous and interesting ways, one can make a compelling argument that Lee is also the consummate, Hollywood-oriented director, his scenes, music and language engaging issues not only driven by the emergence and development of a 'new' black cinema, but also often paying homage to the classic Hollywood cinematic language, style and business strategies. In one of *Do the Right Thing*'s many soliloquies, Radio Raheem steps out from behind the sonic barrier of his radio to energetically act out the story of the struggle between good and evil in a scene that is a tribute to its classic Hollywood precedent, played by Robert Mitchum as a psychotic itinerant preacher in the classic *The Night of the Hunter* (1955).

While out on a delivery, Mookie encounters Radio Raheem in the street and admires his new 'b-boy' knuckle rings, spelling out 'Love' on

the right and 'Hate' on the left hand. At Mookie's compliment, Raheem, directly addressing the up-angle, medium camera shot (which causes him to look down in an intimidating manner on Mookie and the audience) delivers his most eloquent words in the film. 'Let me tell you the story of the Right-Hand–Left-Hand – it's the tale of Good and Evil.' Extending his left fist adorned with the knuckle ring

Charles Laughton's *The Night of the Hunter*

'Hate', Raheem notes that 'it was with this hand Cain iced his brother'.
Then holding up his right fist adorned with 'Love', he comments that
'these five fingers go straight to the soul of man. The hand of Love.' The
look on Raheem's face is animated with a slightly crazed gleam in his
eyes. With 'Fight the Power' reverberating in the background, Radio
Raheem, evoking the boxing metaphor, deftly and excitedly throws
hooks, jabs and crosses at the camera, as one realises that his knuckle
rings, while ostensibly jewellery could as easily turn into 'brass knuckles'.
He tells of the struggle between right and left, with the left hand 'kicking
much ass' until the right comes back and triumphs 'with left hand Hate,
k.o.-ed by Love'.

 The hand-held camera now shifts, framing Raheem looking down at
Mookie in a medium shot from the side; they are facing each other. Raheem
winds up his soliloquy in an edgey, foreboding tone that recalls the pent-up
menace of Robert Mitchum's original brilliant, crazed performance of the
same scene. But now, instead of two runaway children facing the baleful
preacher (Mitchum) it's Mookie, childlike in stature in contrast to the
looming Raheem. Fists clenched and looking down on Mookie, Raheem
solemnly declares 'If I love you, I love you. But if I hate you …' Staring

Homage to Hollywood

deadpan into the pause, Mookie, always the trickster middleman, nonchalantly plays it off with 'There it is, Love and Hate.' Raheem, stirring a subtle undercurrent of relief, then announces 'I love you Mookie.' They shake on it and depart. Again, a sense of tense ambivalence is key to understanding the representational politics of Raheem's most revealing scene. By depicting Raheem as moody and intimidating, neither politically heroic nor even especially likeable, Lee implicitly argues here that an equal standard of justice and human rights should apply to all, whether black urban youth, white, male, female, feared 'suspect' or 'brand name' celebrity. Regardless of how one feels about Raheem, as he confronts and provokes practically all the neighbourhood residents with his radio during the course of the day, he does not deserve to die at the hands of the police, mainly for a state of social perception, being criminalised as a black youth at the bottom of the post-industrial social order and belonging to a formation that is fodder for the prison-industrial complex.[35] One of Lee's principal objections to the way a number of mainstream critics read *Do the Right Thing*'s conclusion, is that they privileged property rights over human rights, with these critics being more distraught over the destruction of 'Sal's Famous Pizzeria' than the loss of human life – Radio Raheem's.[36]

'There it is, Love and Hate'

7

Besides the obvious strategy of advancing African American film-making at the business and industry levels by pursuing and laying claim to auteur status (in the Hollywood sense of rapidly financing and making a series of films that bear his signature as a star persona director), Lee's further engagement with the classic Hollywood style surfaces in his use of distinct moments of the extra-diegetic background music. The use of European or American symphonic music to create lush panoramic soundscapes, or refrains and melodies that add to the seamlessness of Hollywood's classic 'invisible style' whereby traces of a film's production are covered over or erased in the diegesis, occurs in many of Lee's films including *Malcolm X*, but is perhaps most marked in Lee's tribute to basketball and fathers, *He Got Game* (1998). These symphonic moments and undercurrents also occur throughout *Do the Right Thing*, in this case composed by William Lee (Spike Lee's father) in a musical style most akin to Aaron Copland's work, but inflected through the blues-jazz idiom. Most notably we hear these symphonic strains as Mookie navigates the block delivering pizzas and socialising with its residents; or as background to Sal's reflective moments, or behind Da Mayor in his scenes with Mother Sister. Moreover, this extra diegetic background music does further sonic, ideological work in both *He Got Game* and *Do the Right Thing*, in the way it underscores a subtle claim Lee makes for his films to a certain kind of populist, nostalgic Americanness a feeling that is usually associated with Hollywood classic genres, the Western and the musical coming most to mind here. Lee further augments this identification with a sense of nostalgic Americanness, in yet another way with his staging of grand musical, dance performance numbers in both *School Daze* and *Malcolm X*. This claim is further evinced in the latter, where it is literally visualised in the opening credits when the smouldering 'X' of the title shot is templated with the stars and stripes of the American flag. All of these subtle assertions and touches in Lee's films gradually add up, pointing to the broader African American contention that 'blackness' (perhaps as some would argue in a perpetual binary bind and tension with 'whiteness') is the quintessential American experience.

Yet, as with every other aspect of *Do the Right Thing*, the deployment of music is abundantly complex beyond its associations with the formal machinations of the classic Hollywood soundtrack. Lee uses African American music in the film to give multivocal presence to his creative understanding of the 'new blackness', varied black subjectivities and social orientations that encompass a number of black musical genres and traditions. Broadly, this strategy encompasses three loose, and sometimes overlapping, black musical trajectories: commercial jazz-blues as a mainstream idiom; black music as the expression of *Do the Right Thing*'s black historical and cultural agendas; and rap music in the guise of Public Enemy as the resistance music of a new generation of black urban youth. And while the film samples and deploys varied musical styles, even including a scene featuring musical combat between the radios and musics of the neighbourhood's resident Puerto Ricans and Radio Raheem, as he prevails with 'Fight the Power', the thematic focus of the film is ostensibly on African American music. The clearest and most celebratory musical expressions of Lee's claim to being 'a black nationalist with a movie camera' are the choice of rap music's 'Fight the Power' as *Do the Right Thing*'s theme, along with the 'WE LOVE' musical roll call as voice-over to a montage of neighbourhood scenes and characters, broadcast by Mister Senor Love Daddy: 'Thelonious Monk … Miles Davis … Aretha Franklin … Otis Redding … Bessie Smith … Duke Ellington … Sam Cooke … Bob Marley … Cannonball and Nat Adderley … Louis Armstrong … We want to thank you all for making our lives just a little brighter, here on WE LOVE Radio.' While many musics and styles are sampled throughout the film, the roll call voice-over keeps the focus on the African American musical tradition.[37]

In addition, all of the film's black musical currents form the sonic and ideological complement to *Do the Right Thing*'s visual design, this being

Cityscape comparisons:
(bottom) Romare
Bearden, *The Dove*
(© Romare Bearden
Foundation/VAGA, New
York/DACS, London
2001)

evinced by the call for 'AFROCENTRIC bright' colours in the look of the film in Lee's production journal.[38] In marked contrast to the scopic regime of classic Hollywood cinematography which is almost entirely concerned with depicting white skin most favourably at the top of a Manichean hierarchy of light,[39] the films's Afrocentric colours are attentively co-ordinated with its cinematography and lighting to complement and bring out the full range and resonance of brown and black skin tones. Along with the carefully stylised realism of Do the Right Thing's sets, staging and its overall mise-en-scène, these bright hot colours and sepia skin tones visually allude to and remind one most of the cityscapes and brown-skinned people that are the subjects of the collages and paintings of eminent African American painter, the late Romare Bearden. Whether deliberately referenced or linked by culture, history and subject, the scenes of Mother Sister in her window, black and brown people on the porches and congregating in the streets and on corners, the brownstone façades, brick walls, and tangled ironwork of fire-escapes, all cinematically evoke the urban 'folk' ambience, the range and power of many of Bearden's finest works.[40] Bearden's 1985 collage and acrylic The Street, his 1964 collage The Dove, or his 1971 collage The Block are but a few of the examples out of the many that bear striking resonance with the overall mise en scène of Do the Right Thing. This sense of a universal African American visuality, replete with hip-hop fashions and black music, is perhaps one of Do the Right Thing's most significant, and yet hardly remarked upon, contributions to building a mainstream, African American cinema practice that challenges and erodes the skin-colour hierarchy of Hollywood's classic optical hegemony.[41]

8

In other ways Do the Right Thing, and the Spike Lee filmic trajectory are indelibly situated in the history of tangled contentions and debates between black cinematic emergence and Hollywood domination, a principal issue among these struggles being Hollywood's repression of black romance,

intimacy and sexuality on the big screen. Looking back, this structured absence was one of the most salient issues that the Blaxploitation period, albeit problematically, tried to confront and remedy. Kicking off the period, the sexual outlaw Sweetback, of Melvin Van Peebles's *Sweet Sweetback's Baadasssss Song*, in the opinion of several critics, tried to fuck his way to emancipation. And perhaps the most redeeming moment in all of *Superfly*, is the tender, erotic lovemaking scene between Priest (Ron O'Neal) and his girlfriend (Sheila Frazier) in a luxurious sunken bubble bath, surrounded by mirrors. But also

(top) *Sweet Sweetback's Baadasssss Song*: sexual outlaw; (above) *Superfly*: Blaxploitation Eros

the black detective Shaft (Richard Roundtree) in the Gordon Parks directed hit, *Shaft* (1971), has a black girlfriend to satisfy the expectations of cultural nationalism, while demonstrating his 'superspade' macho by sleeping around, having random sex with various attractive white women. But by the mid-to late 70s collapse of the Blaxploitation wave, Hollywood concentrated its attention on the rise of two black stars, Richard Pryor and then Eddie Murphy, while expressions of black romance and sexuality, were, once again, largely banished from the dominant cinema screen.

The mid-80s onset of the new black film wave and a new generation of film-makers, including Julie Dash, Robert Townsend, Matty Rich, John Singleton, and most eminently Spike Lee, coupled with the emergence of a handful of black actors in Hollywood's mainstream features, once again put increasing pressure on the dominant film industry to lift its representational embargo on black romance and sexuality. In the commercial mainstream, Gregory Hines and Lonette McKee demanded that the scenes of black romance under threat of deletion be retained in *The Cotton Club* (1984). Similarly, Whoopi Goldberg openly protested MGM's racism for cutting an interracial love scene between her and the white Sam Elliot in her detective vehicle *Fatal Beauty* (1987). That same year, upon the release of the new black film wave's independent 'guerilla financed' *Hollywood Shuffle* (1987), director-actor Robert Townsend was insistent on structuring a romantic angle, between he and Anne Marie Johnson as his love interest, into the film's story-line. Townsend went on to underscore the point and put the issue in perspective by commenting in an interview that 'this year I'll be the only black man who kisses a black woman on a screen. That's deep.'[42]

However, it was Spike Lee's work, meeting the issues of sex and pleasure head on in his sexual farce and first breakthrough hit *She's Gotta Have It*, that led the impulse of the new black film wave to recuperate black romance and intimacy on the big commercial screen. In *She's Gotta Have It*, Lee takes what could be considered a male perspective on sex and romance and turns it on its head, in that the film focuses on the sexual adventures of a female protagonist, Nola Darling (Tracy Camila Johns), who chooses to live her life as if she had the sexual options of a man. That is to say, Nola simultaneously keeps three male lovers and finally rebels against the confining expectations of all of them. *She's Gotta Have It*'s box-office success launched Lee's commercial career by grossing over $7 million in its first eighteen months of distribution, on an initial investment of $175,000. Since then, Lee has gone on to make the visual representation of black (or black/white) heterosexual pleasure a consistent component, scene, moment, or issue in almost of all of his films. Many critics have argued that Lee's depictions of sex and sexuality are problematic and controversial, to say the least, but as with every other issue in his films, eros, sexual intimacy and visual pleasure are tricky concerns, fraught with ambiguity and contested from many perspectives. For instance, as wry commentary on the fraternity system in *School Daze*, black sex becomes totally objectified with women literally traded as trophies between fraternity brothers. In *Mo' Better Blues*, its musician protagonist Bleek Gilliam (Denzel Washington) keeps two comely women,

while glibly explaining his faithlessness in stark masculinist terms as a 'dick thing'. In *Jungle Fever*, as well as *Malcolm X* and *He Got Game*, interracial romance is cast as suspect and doomed. And yet, in perhaps inadvertent homage to dominant cinema's conventions, in both *Malcolm X* and *Jungle Fever* the erotic allure of female,

Mo' Better Blues

white skin and body are fetishised and offered as forbidden and desired pleasures, barely contained, and further hyping the popular appeal of these films.[43]

The scene in *Do the Right Thing* that marks Lee's commitment to representing black eros and sex as a privileged site of visual pleasure in his work opens when, late in the day, Mookie delivers a pizza to Tina's apartment, this being the only way she can compel Mookie to visit her and pay some attention to his responsibilities as a father and partner. After some verbal banter at the door about the pizza being hot or not, Mookie steps in, and abandoning all pretence tosses the pizza aside, as he and Tina embrace and passionately kiss. The conversation then turns to Mookie's long absences, to which he responds that he's working and 'gettin' paid', but that he can stay 'long enough to do the nasty'. Tina's answer is affectionately playful, but sticks to the issue: 'First of all it's too hot. But if you think I'm gonna let you get some, put your clothes on and not see

Black Eros

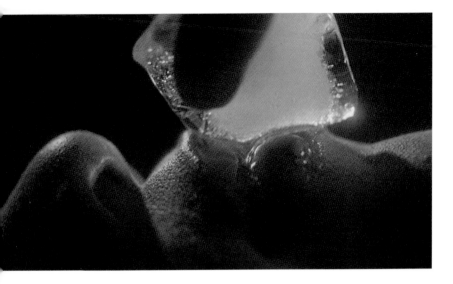

your black ass for another week, you're buggin', o.k.?' Instead of 'doin' the nasty', Mookie then proposes an alternative that marks Lee's idealised celebration and sexualisation of the black female body, as he asks Tina to take her clothes off. But the underlying issue persists, with Tina reminding Mookie that the last time she gave in to him they ended up with a son. Impugning Mookie's role as a father, she adds 'do you remember your son, Hector?' This critique is sustained when Mookie goes into the kitchen for ice cubes; his mother-in-law also berates him for neglecting his son. Then in a series of close-ups, to the passionate slow, soul music of Mister Senor Love Daddy, 'yes children, this is the cool out corner', Mookie, using ice cubes, maps the erotic contours of Tina's sensuous body, as he pays homage: 'Thank God for lips, … the neck, … knees, the right nipple, … the left nipple ….' and so on. The scene ends on a close-up of Mookie and Tina's lips in close amorous, conjunction, when Mookie says he's got to go and Tina warns him that she'll 'kick his ass' if he doesn't return after work.

This erotic ice-cube scene alludes to the best of its Blaxploitation precedents (mainly the *Superfly* bathtub scene), while pushing Lee's 'black nationalist with a camera' agenda to reinscribe black romance and the beauty and eros of the black female body on the big screen. Moreover, the cultural agenda, in this instance foregrounding black partnership, sustains itself in the film in other ways. *Do the Right Thing* plays the young, turbulent, relationship between Tina and Mookie as counter-point to the pairing of the elderly Mother Sister and Da Mayor, a partnership that in itself signifies on multiple levels. In contrast to Tina and Mookie, Mother Sister and Da Mayor represent a surviving older, generational grounding of African American culture and its subtle expressions in the city. Obviously, the names 'Mother Sister' and 'Da Mayor' are imbued with an extended family, community and African American cultural valence. Furthermore, sitting on the front porch, communicating cultural values between black women and across generations, Jade and Mother Sister act

out one of *Do the Right Thing*'s nuanced cultural colloquialisms in the much commented upon 'head scratching' scene, when Jade scratches Mother Sister's scalp and combs her hair while they discuss Da Mayor's reputation and cover recent community events. Significantly, Mother Sister and Da Mayor's relationship also carries powerful extra-diegetic connotations on the screen, in that this is a cameo performance by one of American cinema's most recognised and celebrated black actor couples, Ruby Dee and Ossie Davis, further idealising their pairing in the narrative. The two couples are also linked by juxtaposition in the unfolding of narrative events, with Mother Sister resolving her rejection of Da Mayor in the scene just before Mookie and Tina finally get together for their ice cube scene. And *Do the Right Thing's* explosive conclusion suggests that both couples are on the way to improving their relationships. It is Da Mayor who steps forth to hug and comfort Mother Sister when she emotionally breaks down at the height of the riot scene. And just as Mookie wakes up in bed with Tina and his son on the morning after the conflagration, so Da Mayor wakes up in Mother Sister's bed, she having stayed up all night after being too anxious to sleep. Further validating the generational endurance of black cultural values, the elder couple speculate

Cultural nuance

as to whether the neighbourhood is still standing, with Mother Sister concluding that 'we're still standing.'

9

More than any other issue on *Do the Right Thing*'s complex representational agenda, though, the film's astute and timely focus on police brutality, in all of its attendant, corrupt expressions, will always rank

Idealised couples

it as one of the most socially relevant and prophetic masterpieces of American cinema. At this writing, eleven years after its critically hailed and contentious premiere, the issues that *Do the Right Thing* has most expressly framed and persistently forecast – police brutality, racial profiling and the pervasive, differentially ill, treatment of communities of colour by the nation's police departments – are still stubbornly with us. In a reactionary sense, conservative film critics have been correct to fear racial unrest, once again, spreading across the land; they're just in deep denial, or callously indifferent, as to the enduring structural causes of that unrest. As already argued, history has proven these critics ideologically blind and egregiously wrong about *Do the Right Thing* as the spark or origin of racial rebellion. Rather *Do the Right Thing,* as a creative, socially diagnostic mediation of the nation's failed racial policies and racially skewed criminal justice system, has been cast in the unenviable position of being the bearer of the bad news. Indeed, the police harassment, brutalisation and murder of America's non-white citizens has been an historical pattern and cornerstone of white supremacy dating back at least as far as Emancipation.[44] If anything, *Do the Right Thing*'s resolution is complex and addresses several tendencies, while a call to social justice and political action focused on the then upcoming mayoral race is also a call for social restraint and calm. In the words of Mister Senor Love Daddy's final voice-over, 'the cash money word for the day is "chill".'

Further rebutting charges of incitement to racial violence brought against *Do the Right Thing* in the press, one must note that a full twenty-one years *before* the film's release President Lyndon Johnson's 'Kerner Commission on Civil Disorders' was formed to investigate the root causes of the widespread black urban uprisings of the mid-to late 60s, coming with the decline of the Civil Rights Movement and black people's rising frustration with a system that granted them legal-political rights, but still confined them to social disadvantage and poverty at the bottom of the American economy. These urban rebellions culminated in the fierce period of 1967 through to the end of 1968, with 384 uprisings in 298 cities and especially massive insurrections in Detroit and Newark.[45] Reporting in 1968, the Commission pointedly noted that they had

cited deep hostility between police and ghetto communities as a primary cause of the disorders surveyed by the Commission. In Newark, in Detroit, in Watts, in Harlem – in practically every city that has experienced racial disruption since the summer of 1964 – abrasive relationships between police and Negroes and other minority groups have been a major source of grievance, tension and, ultimately, disorder.'[46]

Since *Do the Right Thing*'s 1989 release, the national media have confirmed that the misconduct and tensions explored in the film, and cited by the Kerner Commission two decades before it, remain largely unchanged, if not unchallenged by black activism. In one of the most egregious cases, 1992 headlines and newscasts were occupied with the saga of the videotaped Rodney King police torture incident, the initial acquittal of the few officers charged and the ensuing rebellion of a broad spectrum of Los Angeles' residents, in outrage at the injustice of this verdict.

And the news continues to be consistently bad, punctuated with an unending series of suspicious deaths of people of colour at police hands, including Jonny Gamage in Pittsburgh, Earl Faizon in New Jersey, Patrick Dorismond and Anthony Baez in NYC, to name but a few high-profile cases that have had media coverage in the 90s. Moreover, New Jersey has been embroiled in a series of lawsuits, protests and legal actions aimed at ending the state's 'racial profiling', the practice by which the police have effectively viewed and treated non-white citizens as 'guilty until proven otherwise'. But perhaps the cases most recently disturbing to New Yorkers on what has been a long, ongoing list, are the death of Ammadou Diallo, an unarmed African immigrant, who died in a hail of forty-one police

bullets while he was standing, as a 'suspect', in the entrance of his apartment building; and also the brutal sodomy and torture of Abner Louima in a Brooklyn police station bathroom. A seemingly cyclical and permanent social dynamic is at work here, going from a publicised, brutal police action, to open protest and revolt, to state promises of investigation and change, to a social lull, and then starting all over again with another extra-judicial police murder of some unlucky victim of colour. At this writing, in the first year of the new century, I can hardly keep up with the headlines, as the city of Cincinnati has been wracked after three days of protest and rebellion over the police killing of black teenager Timothy Thomas, wanted for traffic warrants. Nor will this list end, as long as police brutality is used as one of the many instruments to maintain America's *de facto* (and *de jure*) system of racial oppression and white privilege.[47] And 'that's the triple truth, Ruth' as Mister Senor Love Daddy says.

In light of this grim historical pattern of injustice, what is interesting about *Do the Right Thing* is the relative equity that Lee gives to depicting the circumstances surrounding police misconduct from the multiple perspectives in the film's culminating disaster. As with all issues in the film, the riot that closes it is not one-dimensionally simplistic. Rather, it is constructed as an accelerating cascade of violent events imbued with contradiction and ambivalence that spins out of everyone's control, ending with results nobody wants and lots of questions as to what exactly is 'the right thing' to do. While the film is clear on its stance against police

Protesting Diallo's death

brutality, the need to unseat Mayor Koch and for social justice and change in the police department and community, the insurrection depicted here is a chaotic 'no win' event revealed from many uneasy angles. As *Do the Right Thing*'s day fades to night, the three most erratic characters of the story world gather in an alley, the only supporters of the impending boycott of 'Sal's'. Again, as in other scenes, this tableau is interwoven with multiple, sometimes contending images and discourses. Consistent with Lee's intent that the film be used as a political instrument in the upcoming mayoral election, the wall behind the trio is covered with 'Dump Koch' graffiti, torn Jesse Jackson 'Get Out The Vote' posters, while 'Fight the Power' blares from Raheem's radio. Yet the most, seemingly, political voices in the diegesis are also the most reflexively strident and unstable. Tellingly, the black voice of a tenant in one of the buildings facing the alley yells for them to 'cut out that rap music ...' to which Raheem, Buggin Out and Smiley yell back in sequence, 'Yo, I'll fuck you up ... once, ... twice ... three times!' Predictably, Spike Lee's politicos are not especially likeable, nor do they conform to white, middle-class norms, or a particular community or cultural standard. However, their issues and grievances are real, and as black urban youth, they continually seek to vocalise and

'Yo, I'll fuck you up'

redress these issues, no matter how unevenly, in various modalities from consuming hip-hop brand name fashions and music, to linguistic, theatrical and sometimes violent protest. Thus, the fuse is lit for the conflagration to come.

Meanwhile, it's closing time at 'Sal's Famous' and the atmosphere is one of general relief with Sal exuding satisfaction at the profits from a 'great, great day'. In a *Godfather* parody that subtly runs throughout the movie, Sal, waving a fist full of money, declares that 'there's nothing like a family working together'. Sal rambles on, gushing with naive paternalism and proclaiming that he's thinking of renaming the pizzeria, 'Sal & Sons …' in honour of Vito and Pino, an honour extended to Mookie, whom Sal says he also thinks of 'as a son'. Marking the tensions and conflicts of a long hot work day, and in answer to Sal, the camera slowly pans, close-up, registering the tired, skeptical looks of all three 'sons', as they gaze back at Sal in sullen disbelief. Mookie wants to 'get paid', and all want to pack it up for the evening, when the neighbourhood's teenage quartet bangs on the door requesting 'one last slice', words that will soon prove to be ironically literal. Over the objections of Mookie who wants to go home, Sal admits them and by doing so, admits disaster.

In rush Buggin Out, Raheem and Smiley, with Raheem's radio turned up full volume, blasting 'Fight the Power' and Buggin Out screaming over the music for representation, for some black people on that 'motherfuckin' wall of fame, now!' People are usually brought down by their lapses or minor faults. And while Sal is portrayed as one of the most humanised and reasonable characters throughout the film (something Lee has taken critical heat for) the scene quickly escalates with Sal grabbing his baseball bat from under the counter. Facing Raheem and Buggin Out's provocations for the second time that day, Sal's good-natured paternal persona quickly cracks and out comes a screed of racist invective about 'jungle music', accompanied by egregious racial profanities, the likes of 'black cocksucker', 'nigger motherfucker', and so on. At this point the conflict is verbal, but

again, Lee makes one of his principal points about the play and use of both profane and civil language throughout the film: the poetic creative uses of vibrant urban vernacular and the cursing, signifyin', put-down style known as 'the dozens' can quickly devolve into hate speech exploding from everyone's racial id, over the most trivial of matters, especially at the end of a long, hot day. The music and shouts escalate until Sal finally loses it and smashes Raheem's radio to pieces with his bat. A line is crossed here, from

Sonic explosion

Force out of control

words to physical action. The camera pans around the pizzeria, recording shocked faces as all fall into a stunned silence which is quickly broken when Raheem drags Sal over the counter and starts to throttle him. All weigh in to a confused brawl that rolls out into the street, where neighbourhood spectators and police arrive and join in.

Deploying the infamous, and all too often fatal, police 'choke hold', four struggling cops pull Raheem off Sal and subdue him, as the residents of the neighbourhood look on, yelling to restrain the cops. In a gruesome metonym for lynching, the camera cuts to a close-up shot of Raheem's sneaker-clad feet, lifted dangling, off the ground. One of the cops shouts to the others '… that's enough', finally realising that things have gone too far. But it's too late for Raheem, and in a close-up, he falls to the street, face down, eyes open … dead. In a panic resembling a platoon whose mission has gone bad, the cops retreat and cover up the incident by taking Raheem's body with them. The crowd responds with swelling anger. 'It's murder … Just like Eleanor Bumpers. Michael Stewart.' 'Damn, it ain't even safe in our own neighborhood.' 'It never was.' ML and Sweet Dick Willie of the corner men speak up. 'It's as plain as day. They didn't have to kill the boy.' The crowd's anger is raw and openly expressed. Someone yells 'He died because he had a radio.' Registering a numb expression, Mookie, is shocked out of his slick negotiating middleman guise as he moves away from Sal and his sons. He then vents his anger at Raheem's death and rejects minimum wage servitude on the 'pizza plantation', by screaming 'hate' and throwing a trash can through Sal's window, touching off the neighbourhood charge to loot and burn 'Sal's Famous'. As the pizzeria is trashed, Smiley – very much a child playing with matches – sets the place on fire. Then comes a portentous montage, Dante's cinematic inferno as 'Sal's' burns. The flickering light of the conflagration reflects off the pictures on Sal's exclusive, Italian and Italian American, 'Wall of Fame'. Cast in a red glow of dancing flames, the camera pans in close-up over the portraits of the eminent, the beautiful and the famous – Al Pacino, Sophia

(top) 'Raheem is dead!'; (middle) from fame to flame; (bottom) contested representation

Loren, John Travolta, Frank Sinatra. All are consumed in the fire, thus making the obvious and conclusive point that such fixed, monolithic visions of race and culture can no longer reign, or even survive in a multicultural neighbourhood, community, or world.

But now, debates about representational multiculturalism and definitions of racial identity take on even more ominous and urgent complications as the crowd, exuberant from burning 'Sal's', grows uglier: it's the Korean grocer's turn. Led by ML of the corner men, the neighbourhood crowd, now an angry mob, surrounds the Korean grocery store. In near panic, store owner Sonny swings a broom, making an energetic argument for neighbourhood solidarity and the social construction of 'race', proclaiming 'I'm no white. I'm no white. I'm black. I'm black. You, me ... the same.' ML confronts Sonny, wanting to argue the issue of what exactly constitutes *blackness*: the shared experience of discrimination, or culture and racial identity. The mob, while not entirely agreeing with the fine points of Sonny's thesis, does appreciate his sincere, if belated, grasp of racial 'double consciousness'; they laugh in sarcasm and with relief. The tension and anger are momentarily broken, and Cocoanut Sid steps forward advising the crowd that the Korean is OK, 'leave him alone'.

At this moment, with the crowd milling and restless, *Do the Right Thing*'s stylised, staged look, its comedy and poetic realism all give way. Now these tropes are complicated and inflected through the lens of historical allusion. The pandemonium and social chaos explode as the police and fire departments return, ostensibly to defend private property, to fight the fire at 'Sal's' but end up fighting the neighbourhood. The film's riotous *mise-en-scène* references 60s newsreel footage depicting the violence of the Civil Rights Movement and the urban Black Power rebellions that followed. And there's a sense here that the same issues fought over in the Civil Rights Movement, social equality and justice, have persistently lingered, having never really gone away. In Lee's own words,

'Now we've come full circle. We're back to Montgomery or Birmingham, Alabama. The only thing missing is Sheriff Bull Connor and the German shepherds.'[48] As protesters are hosed down by the firemen, and the police chase and arrest looters, Mookie and his sister Jade sit on the curb watching the spectacle and absurdity of it all in silent dejection. Their looks are mirrored by Sal, Vito and Pino, also dismayed and silently watching from a safe distance. The riot sequence ends on an overtly political gesture, with Smiley re-entering the burned-out shell of the pizzeria and tacking up the postcard of 'Malcolm and Martin'. For a brief, ironic moment, to the theme music of 'Fight the Power', the 'Wall of Fame' – a ruin looking like the set in a war movie – is finally integrated.

The shattered equilibrium of the neighbourhood, and narrative, is somewhat restored with the dawn of a new, hot, hot, day. The mood is set by the reflective, orchestrated blues-jazz idiom of the soundtrack, and the camera's slow crawl down the pavement scanning the garbage, litter, broken furniture, abandoned sneakers, all of the burnt jetsam and flotsam that remains of 'Sal's Famous'. The voice most clearly identified with the

'No justice, no peace!'

film's overall stance and values comes on the air at WE LOVE Radio. Consistent with *Do the Right Thing*'s persistence as an open-ended, unresolved text vocalising issues and diagnosing problems, asking questions rather than posing smug answers in the style of the classic Hollywood ending, the voice asks two salient questions posed as an ellipsis. Mister Senor Love Daddy poetically comments in his wake-up call: 'My people, my people, what can I say ... say what I can. ... Are we going to live together. Together are we going to live?' Do we have the will as a people to achieve social equality in our power relations and can we survive our inevitable multiculturalism? With this wake up call comes Lee's note endorsing rebuilding black cultural and family relations. Da Mayor wakes up at Mother Sister's place and Mookie wakes up in bed with Tina and his son. However, the day's agenda is pressing and consistent with his 'get paid' focus, Mookie jumps out of bed to go have one final meeting with Sal, as he says, to 'get my money'.

Mookie finds Sal totally depressed, sitting on the steps of his burned-out pizzeria. Their meeting is not pleasant, and both feel the need to emotionally vent, as they argue back and forth about 'getting paid' the cost of the window Mookie broke – property vs. human rights – and who was at fault for the preceding night's carnage. Mookie interjects 'motherfuck a window, Radio Raheem is dead' to which Sal sarcastically replies, 'I know he's dead. I was here, remember?' After more back and forth blaming, Mookie lets Sal know that he's aware that Sal will 'get over' on the insurance for the place, to which Sal responds with a long rant about ownership and having built 'Sal's Famous'. Finally, in one of the film's memorable, classic scenes, Sal takes five $100 bills wads them up and throws them at Mookie, who stands dead-pan as they bounce off his skinny chest. Mookie picks the bills up and, reversing the gesture throws two of them back, to bounce off of the considerably more corpulent Sal. Mookie explains that his salary is 'two-fitty' a week and that he owes Sal $50. In a moment very much visually symbolic of America's racial condition and expressing the contentious and comic ambience of the film, Mookie and Sal stand mute, in a face-off, in discursive, racial, economic stalemate. Black–white, worker–boss, youth–senior, African American–Italian American, their differences are seemingly unresolvable. Yet at this time, in this nation, it is impossible for them to live apart (as in the social disaster of *apartheid*). We are reminded of Mister Senor Love Daddy's final, elliptical question. Both have their pride, yet neither wants to leave two 'C notes' on the pavement. Again, it's back

'Gotta get paid'

and forth, kids in a school-yard, 'Keep it.' 'No, you keep it.' 'No, you keep it.' They try to find a way to part amicably, finally turning to the weather to open up communication – 'another hot day'. Then, as they turn to part Sal asks Mookie what he's going to do with himself. In a layered, double answer we hear Mookie the b-boy survivalist, but also echoes of Spike Lee the director arguing the material necessity of film-making, as Mookie emphatically responds that he's going to 'make that money. Get paid.' The two exchange poignant silent looks. Then in a quick gesture of compromise, perhaps considering this his separation package, Mookie picks up the two $100 bills from the pavement and departs.

With the previous night's uprising already starting to fade, the camera pulls slowly back to an overview of the block as a game of pick-up ball starts in the street and the community commences the routines of yet another hot, hot day. In an overt act of political triangulation, *Do the Right Thing* gives its last comments to the three most reliant personas in the film – Mister Senor Love Daddy, Dr Martin Luther King and Malcolm X. In the final voice-over, Mister Senor Love Daddy sarcastically reports the news, implicitly recognising the cyclical nature of the previous night's violent events, and that the political apparatus that maintains the racial status quo is already in full play. As Mister Senor Love Daddy reports it, the Mayor is going to appoint a 'blue ribbon' panel to look into last night's disturbances and 'will not tolerate property being destroyed by anyone'. Yet resistance always answers oppression, and *Do the Right Thing*'s imaginative story world merges with the film's real world historicity and political instrumentality. In anticipation of that season's Koch versus Dinkins contest, Mister Senor Love Daddy says, 'Register to vote, the election is coming up', then fade to black.

Culminating the visual motif that has recurred throughout the film, two quotes roll up on the screen: one from Martin and the other from Malcolm. In the first quote Dr Martin Luther King speaks of the futility of violence as a way to achieve racial justice, because of the mutual

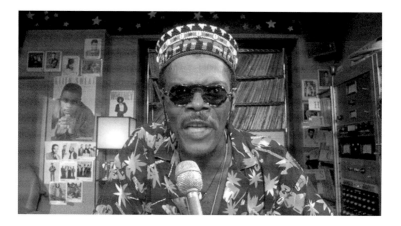

destruction it causes and the bitterness and brutality it engenders in oppressed and oppressor alike. Second, a quote by Malcolm X remarks on the structural nature of racism, noting that while there are lots of good people in America, it seems that the bad people have all the power, and that under these circumstances 'self-defense' is not violence, but rather 'intelligence'. Then comes a sustained, full-screen close-up of the postcard we've only fleetingly glimpsed throughout the film, 'Martin and Malcolm' smiling and shaking hands. In a rather obvious way, the juxtaposition of these two martyrs and their words comments on the long, slow, historical oscillation of black social thought and political movements between the poles of integration and separation. While these quotes are by no means mutually exclusive, they also resonate with the DuBoisian notion of 'double consciousness' by which blacks in America continually feel their 'twoness – an American, a Negro, two souls, two thoughts, two unreconciled strivings; two warring ideals in one dark body ...'. Director Spike Lee further underscores the theme of 'twoness' in black American politics and thought, noting in the Epilogue to his production journal that 'in the end justice will prevail one way or another. There are two paths to that. The way of King or the way of Malcolm.'[49] As argued throughout this

'Together, are we going to live?'

essay, *Do the Right Thing* is an open and unresolved text, meant to challenge and disturb the viewer with relevant questions, rather than provide smug, predictable answers that paper over or maintain the starkly unequal power relation between America's whites and its black and non-white *others*. So perhaps we should end by bringing it back to the importance of the death of Radio Raheem as emphasised by the film's final proclamation, a dedication to the real-time fallen victims of racial injustice: Eleanor Bumpers, Michael Griffith, Arthur Miller, Edmund Perry, Yvonne Smallwood and Michael Stewart. At this writing, a dozen years after its premiere, perhaps the real tragedy of *Do the Right Thing* is that all of its issues are still so socially relevant, and that given present conditions in America, the film's closing dedication, a list of the fallen, has no foreseeable end.

Martin and Malcolm

Notes

1 Spike Lee and Lisa Jones, *Do the Right Thing: A Spike Lee Joint* (New York: Simon & Schuster Inc., 1989), p. 50.

2 Spike Lee, 'I Am Not an Anti-Semite', *The New York Times*, 22 August 1990, Op Ed Page, p. 19; Spike Lee, ed., *Five for Five: The Films of Spike Lee* (New York: Stewart, Tabori & Chang, 1991), p. 16.

3 Ed Guerrero, 'Spike Lee and the Fever in the Racial Jungle', in Jim Collins, Hilary Radner, Ava Preacher Collins (eds), *Film Theory Goes to the Movies* (New York: Routledge, 1993) pp. 170–81; Spike Lee and Henry Louis Gates Jr., 'The Final Cut', *Transition,* vol. 0 no. 52 (1991), pp. 194–6.

4 Amiri Baraka, 'Malcolm as Ideology', in Joe Wood (ed.) *Malcolm X: In Our Own Image* (New York: St Martin's Press, 1992); bell hooks, 'Male Heroes and Female Sex Objects: Sexism in Spike Lee's *Malcolm X*', in 'By Any Reviews Necessary: A symposium on *Malcolm X*', in *Cineaste* vol. 19, no. 4, pp. 13–15; Henry Louis Gates Jr, 'Just Whose Malcolm Is It Anyway?' *The New York Times,* 31 May 1992.

5 Spike Lee and Ralph Wiley, *By Any Means Necessary: The Trial and Tribulations of the Making of Malcolm X* (New York: Hiperion, 1992).

6 Herman Gray, 'Cultural Politics as Outrage(ous)', in *Black Renaissance Noire*, vol. 3 no. 1, Fall 2000, pp 92–101.

7 Lee and Jones, *Do the Right Thing,* pp. 62–3, 79; Spike Lee (ed.), *Five for Five,* p. 12.

8 Stanley Crouch, 'Do the Race Thing', *Village Voice*, 20 June 1989.

9 Dan Streible, 'Race and the Reception of Jack Johnson Fight Films', in Daniel Bernardi (ed.), *The Birth of Whiteness, Race and the Emergence of U.S. Cinema*, (New Brunswick, NJ: Rutgers University Press, 1996) pp. 170–200.

10 Joe Klein, 'Spiked? Dinkins and *Do the Right Thing*', *New York*, 26 June 1989, pp. 14–15; David Denby, 'He's Gotta Have It', *New York*, 26 June 1989, pp. 53–4.

11 Lee and Jones, *Do the Right Thing,* p. 76.

12 Vincent F. Rocchio, *Reel Racism: Confronting Hollywood's Construction of Afro-American Culture,* (Boulder, CO: Westview Press, 2001), p. 153; Sharon Willis, *High Contrast: Race and Gender in Contemporary Hollywood Film* (Durham, NC and London: Duke University Press, 1997) pp. 163–5.

13 Lee and Gates Jr, 'The Final Cut', p. 180.

14 S. Craig Watkins, *Representing: Hip-Hop Culture and the Production of Black Cinema* (Chicago, IL: University of Chicago Press, 1998), pp. 107–16; Lee and Gates Jr, 'The Final Cut', pp.178–9.

15 Watkins, *Representing,* pp. 120–3.

16 Lee and Jones, *Do the Right Thing*, p. 57.

17 'Big Rental Films of 1989 in U.S.–Canada,' *Variety*, 24 January 1990, p. 24.

18 Leo Braudy, 'Genre: The Conventions of Connection', in Leo Braudy and Marshall Cohen (eds), *Film Theory and Criticism: Introductory Readings* (New York: Oxford University Press, 1999), p. 613.

19 Gene Siskel, 'This Picture's as good as *The Godfather*', *Chicago Tribune*, 25 June 1989; Vincent Canby, 'Spike Lee Tackles Racism In *Do The Right Thing*', *The New York Times*, 30 June 1989, Section C, p. 16.

20 Thomas Doherty, *Do The Right Thing*, in *Film Quarterly*, 43 (2) 1989, pp. 35–40.

21 W.E.B. DuBois, 'Criteria for Negro Art', *The Crisis*, vol. 32, October 1926, p. 292.

22 Robert Stam, 'Bakhtin, Polyphony, and Ethnic/Racial Representation', in Lester D. Friedman (ed.), *Unspeakable Images: Ethnicity and the American Cinema* (Chicago, IL: University of Chicago Press, 1991), p. 259.

23 Rocchio, *Reel Racism*, p. 163.

24 Joe Wood, 'The New Blackness', in Wood (ed.), *Malcolm X*.

25 George Lipsitz, *The Possessive Investment in Whiteness: How White People Profit from Identity Politics* (Philadelphia, PA: Temple University Press, 1998), p. 15. Lipsitz sums up neo-racism nicely saying:

> Attacking the civil rights tradition serves many functions for neoconservatives. By mobilising existing racisms and generating new ones, neoconservatives seek to discredit the egalitarian and democratic social movements of the post-World War II era and to connect the attacks by those movements on wealth, special privilege, and elite control over education and opportunity to despised and unworthy racial 'others'.

26 Nathan McCall, *Makes Me Wanna Holler: A Young Black Man in America* (New York: Random House, 1994), pp. 104–5.

27 Ed Guerrero, 'Black Violence as Cinema: From Cheap Thrills to Historical Agonies', in J. David Slocum (ed.), *Violence and American Cinema* (New York: Routledge, 2001) pp. 211–25.

28 The racial income gap is perhaps the best index of black 'progress' in a nation in which social equality is so dependent upon what one owns. As Andrew Hacker notes, in 1975 blacks earned $605 for every $1,000 that whites earned; by 1995 that figure had dropped to a black $577 for every white $1,000. Andrew Hacker, *Money: Who Has How Much and Why* (New York: Scribner, 1997), pp. 146–7.

29 Thomas C. Holt, *The Problem of Race in the 21st Century*, (Cambridge, MA: Harvard University Press, 2000), pp. 84–5.

30 The 'new black film wave' started in the mid-80s with the breakthrough work of a cohort of young black film-makers – the likes of Spike with *She's Gotta Have It*, Robert Townsend with *Hollywood Shuffle*, Matty Rich with *Straight Outta Brooklyn* (1991) and Julie Dash with *Daughters of the Dust* (1991). All of these film-makers deployed variations on the theme of 'guerilla financing', i.e., raising their own production money 'by any means necessary' to make their films and crack the discriminatory insider networks and investment ceilings that kept blacks shut out of the production end of the movie business after the collapse of the Blaxploitation period in the mid-70s.

31 Robert Stam, *Film Theory, An Introduction* (Malden, MA: Blackwell, 2000) p. 53; Susan Hayward, *Key Concepts in Cinema Studies* (London and New York: Routledge, 1996), p. 71.

32 Mary Ann Doane, 'The Voice in the Cinema: The Articulation of Body and Space', in Philip Rosen (ed.), *Narrative, Apparatus, Ideology, A Film Theory Reader* (New York: Columbia University Press, 1986), pp. 39–40. Here Doane's observations about cinematic voice and space are consonant with Lee's Brechtian moments when she says that 'if a character looks at and speaks to the spectator, this constitutes an acknowledgment that the character is seen and heard in a radically different space and is therefore generally read as transgressive'.

33 Lee and Jones, *Do the Right Thing*, pp. 63–4. Lee's vision of the economic bottom is clearly broader than 'race'. As for Pino and Vito, Lee says they 'only made it through high school. They will work in their father's pizzeria probably for the rest of their lives and are ill-equipped to do otherwise.' Lee goes on to make the point saying that 'Pino, Vito and Mookie have many similarities. All three are high school graduates and are stuck in dead-end jobs. They are trapped. They would never discuss it amongst themselves', pp. 49–50.

34 Rocchio, *Reel Racism,* pp. 161–3; Derrick Bell, *Faces at the Bottom of the Well: The Permanence of Racism (*New York: Basic Books, 1992), pp. 7–10; Wahneema Lubiano (ed.), *The House That Race Built*, (New York: Vintage Books, 1998), p. vii. Perhaps Lubiano puts it most succinctly, saying that:

> the United States is not just the domicile of a historically specific form of racial oppression, but it sustains itself as a structure through that oppression. If race ... didn't exist, the United States' severe inequalities and betrayal of its formal commitments to social equality and social justice would be readily apparent to anyone existing on this ground.

35 Robin D.G. Kelly, 'Kickin' Reality, Kickin' Ballistics: Gangsta rap and Postindustrial Los Angeles', in William Eric Perkins (ed.),

Droppin' Science, Critical Essays on Rap Music and Hip-Hop Culture (Philadelphia, PA: Temple University Press, 1996), pp. 134–5. Here Kelly puts often recited statistics clearly: 'The criminalization of black male bodies produces and is produced by the shockingly high incarceration rates of African American men ... In 1989, 23 percent of black males ages twenty to twenty-nine were either behind bars or on legal probation or parole.' Kelly goes on to note that studies have provided 'substantial evidence' that black and latino men receive longer sentences, on average, than white men for the same crime.

36 Spike Lee (ed.), *Five for Five,* p. 15. Lee's own words on this point are interesting.

> For me, this film was the litmus test: You could actually tell which critics were closet redneck racist peckerwoods. That whole litany about whether Mookie did or didn't do the right thing was a joke. Some of these critics were more concerned about Sal's Pizzeria burning down than they were with a human life – a black human life. But then again, maybe they didn't consider Radio Raheem human but had neatly relegated him to subhuman, a wilding animal – *exactly like all young black males are.*

37 For an interesting, overall discussion of Lee's use of music in *Do the Right Thing,* see Victoria E. Johnson, 'Polyphony and Cultural Expression – Interpreting Musical Tradition in *Do The Right Thing*', *Film Quarterly*, vol. 47 no. 2, Winter 1993, pp. 18–29.

38 Lee and Jones, *Do the Right Thing*, p. 29.

39 Richard Dyer, *White* (New York: Routledge, 1997), pp. 82–145.

40 Mary Schmidt Campbell, 'History and the Art of Romare Bearden', in *Memory and Metaphor: The Art of Romare Bearden, 1946–1987,* The Studio Museum in Harlem (New York: Oxford University Press, 1991), pp. 7–17.

41 Certainly Lee is acutely aware of the overall politics of colour difference, as he poses it as one of the principal themes in *School Daze* in the cultural struggle between the dark-skinned 'Jigaboos' and the light-skinned 'Wannabees'.

42 Adore Collier, 'Why Hollywood Ignores Black Love and Intimacy', *Ebony*, April 1989, pp. 42–3; ''Fatal Beauty' Love Scene Cut; Goldberg Cites Racism', *Jet*, 2 March 1987, p. 63; Clarence Waldron, 'Robert Townsend Explains Why He Produced Hit Comedy Film, "Hollywood Shuffle"', *Jet*, 1 June 1987, p. 60.

43 Richard Dyer, *Heavenly Bodies: Film Stars and Society* (New York: St Martin's Press, 1986) pp. 42–4; Guerrero, 'Spike Lee and the Fever in the Racial Jungle', pp. 170–81.

44 Derrick Bell, 'Police Brutality: Portent of Disaster and Discomforting Divergence', in Jill Nelson (ed.), *Police Brutality* (New York: W.W. Norton, 2000), pp. 88–101.

45 Ed Guerrero, *Framing Blackness* (Philadelphia PA: Temple University Press, 1993), p. 71; Michael Omi and Howard Winant, *Racial Formation in The United States: From the 1960's to the 1980's* (New York: Routledge and Kegan Paul, 1986), p. 96.

46 *Report for the National Advisory Commission on Civil Disorders* (New York: E.P. Dutton, 1968), pp. 299, 305. But also for the very latest thinking and writing on police brutality see the excellent volume: Nelson (ed.), *Police Brutality.*

47 Bell, 'Police Brutality: Portent of Disaster and Discomforting Divergence', pp. 88–101; Ian Lopez, *White by Law: The Legal Construction of Race in America* (New York: New York University Press, 1998); Guerrero, *Framing Blackness*, p.71: 'The violence peaked between 1967 and 1968 with 384 uprisings in 298 cities …'.

48 Lee and Jones, *Do the Right Thing*, p. 253.

49 W.E.B. DuBois, *The Souls of Black Folk* (New York: Penguin Books, 1996), p. 5; Lee and Jones, *Do the Right Thing*, p. 282.

Credits

DO THE RIGHT THING

USA
1989

Director
Spike Lee
Producer
Spike Lee
Writer
Spike Lee
Photography
Ernest Dickerson
Editor
Barry Alexander Brown
Production Design
Wynn Thomas
Original Music Score
Bill Lee

©Universal City Studios, Inc.
Production Company
A Forty Acres and a Mule
Filmworks production
A Spike Lee Joint

Co-producer
Monty Ross
Line Producer
Jon Kilik
Production Supervisor
Preston Holmes
Auditor
Holly Chase
Assistant Auditor
Eric Oden
Production Comptroller
Robert Nickson
**Forty Acres Production
Co-ordinator**
Susan D. Fowler
**Production Office
Co-ordinator**
Lillian Pyles
**Assistant Production
Office Co-ordinator**
Robin Downes
Unit Manager
R.W. Dixon
Location Manager
Brent Owens
**Forty Acres Production
Assistant**
Audra C. Smith
**Production Assistants –
Set**
Kenny Buford, Spencer
Charles, Eric Daniel, Michael
Ellis, Eddie Joe, Stephanie
Jones, Erik Night, Frederick
Nielsen, Kia Puriefoy, Bruce
Roberts, Dale Watkins
**Production Assistants –
Office**
Steve Burnett,
Judith Norman

Interns
Richard Beaumont, Kai
Bowe, Dawn Cain, Fritz
Celestin, Melissa A. Clark,
Arlene Donnelly, Juliette
Harris, Ernie Mapp, Mitchell
Marchand, Jacki Newson,
Traci Proctor, Sara Renaud,
Carolyn Rouse, Astrid Roy,
Sharoya N. Smalls, Alan C.
Smith, Susan Stuart, Karen
Taylor, Jean Warner, Latanya
White, Gail White, Monique
Williams
First Assistant Director
Randy Fletcher
**Second Assistant
Director**
Nandi Bowe
**2nd Second Assistant
Director**
Chris Lopez
Script Supervisor
Joe Gonzalez
Casting
Robi Reed
Casting Assistant
Andrea Reed
Extras Casting
Sarah Hyde-Hamlet
**Production Assistant –
Casting**
Tracy Vilar
Camera Operator
John Newby
**Additional Camera
Operators**
Frank Prinzi, George Pattison
First Assistant Camera
Jonathan Burkhart

2nd Assistant Camera
Darnell Martin
Additional Camera Assistants
Robert Gorelick,
Paul S. Reuter
Key Grip
Robert Ippolito
Best Boy
Paul Wachter
Dolly Grip
Rex North
3rd Grip
Rodney Bauer
Additional Grips
John Archibald, Erich
Augenstein, Donald Bailer,
Roger Kimpton
Grip Trainee
Marcus Turner
Louma Crane Technician
Stuart Allen
Gaffer
Charles Houston
Best Boy
Val Desalvo
3rd Electrics
Sergei Mihajlov,
John O'Malley
Generator Operator
Derrick Still
Electrics
James Boorman,
Christopher Vanzant
Electric Trainees
Addison Cook, Juan Lopez
Production Assistant – Electric
Beverly C. Jones

Camera Equipment
Technological Cinevideo
Services, Inc.
Stills Photography
David Lee
Special Effects
Steve Kirshoff
Assistant Effects
John N. Berry, Wilfred
Caban, Paul Collangello,
Dave Fletcher, Bill Harrison,
Don Hewitt, William Van Der
Putten, Dennis Zack
Assistant Editor
Tula Goenka
Apprentice Editor
Leander Sales
Art Department Co-ordinator
Pam Stephens
Leadman
Scott Rosenstock
Assistant Art Directors
Michael Green,
Dennis Bradford
Set Decorator
Steve Rosse
Assistant Set Decorator
Jon Rudo
Key Set Dresser
Keith Wall
Set Dressers
Anthony Baldasare, Michael
Lee Benson, James Bilz,
Thomas Hudson Reeve
Scenic Artists
Patricia Bases, Lawrence
Casey, Jeff Miller
2nd Scenic Artist
Joyce Kubalak

Storyboard Artist
Jeff Balsmeyer
Chargeman
Jeffrey L. Glave
Property Master
Octavio Molina
1st Assistant Props
Mark Selemon
2nd Assistant Props
Marc Henry Johnson
3rd Assistant Props
Kevin Ladson
Additional Assistant Props
Andy Lassman
Shop Person
Rosalie Russino
Production Assistant – Shop
Sherman Benjamin
Construction Co-ordinator
Martin Bernstein
Construction Grips
James Bonice, David
Bromberg, Jonathan
Graham, Rich Kerekes,
Charles Marroquin,
Monique Mitchell,
Carl Peterson, Carl Prinzi,
Bryan Unger
Production Assistant – Construction
Robert Woods Jr
Key Set Builder
Ken Nelson
Carpenters
Rodney Clark, Dominic
Ferrar, Harold Horn, Timothy

Main, Chris Miller, Twad
Schuetrum
Costumes
Ruth Carter
**Assistant Costume
Designer**
Karen Perry
Wardrobe Supervisor
Jennifer Ruscoe
Wardrobe Seamstress
Valerie A. Gladstone
**Production Assistants –
Wardrobe**
Michele Boissiere,
Millicent Shelton
Make-up
Matiki Anoff
Additional Make-up
Marianna Najjar
Hair
Larry Cherry
**Main/End Titles
Designed and
Produced by**
Balsmeyer and Everett, Inc.
Do the Right Thing
Logo by
Art Sims/11:24 Design &
Advertising
Opticals
Select Effects
Music Performed by
*The Natural Spiritual
Orchestra*
Conductor:
William J.E. Lee
Tenor and Soprano
Saxophone:
Branford Marsalis

Trumpets:
Terrence Blanchard,
Marlon Jordan
Alto Saxophone:
Donald Harris
Drums:
Jeff 'Tain' Watts
Bass:
Robert Hurst
Pianos:
Kenny Barron, James
Williams
Violins – Contractor:
Stanley G. Hunte
Violins – Concert Master:
Alen W. Sanford
Violins:
Elliot Rodoff, Kenneth
Gordon, John Pintavalle,
Gerald Tarack, Charles
Libove, Louann Montesi,
Paul Peabody, Lewis Eley,
Regis Iandiorio, Sandra
Billingslea, Cecelia A.
Hobbs, Marion J. Pinheiro,
Richard Henrickson,
Joseph Malin, Lesa Terry,
Laura J. Smith, Diane
Monroe, Alvin E. Rodgers,
Elena Barere, Patmore
Lewis, Gregory Komar,
Winterton Garvey
Violas:
Alfred V. Brown, Harry
Zaratzian, Barry Finclair,
Maxine Roach, John R.
Dexter, Lois E. Martin,
Maureen Gallagher,
Juliette Hassner

Cellos:
Frederick Zlotkin, Mark Orrin
Shuman, Bruce Rogers,
Melissa Meel, Eileen M.
Folsom, Zela Terry, Carol
Buck, Astrid Schween
Bass:
Michael M. Fleming,
Rufus Reid
Music Copyist
James 'Jasso' Ware
Piano Tuner
Alexander Ostrovsky
Music Editor
Alex Steyermark
Music Score Recorded at
RCA Studios, New York
Soundtrack
'Fight the Power' by Carlton
Ridenhour, Hank Shocklee,
Eric Sadler, Keith Shocklee,
performed by Public Enemy;
'Don't Shoot Me' by Spike
Lee, Mervyn Warren, Claude
McKnight, David Thomas,
performed by Take 6; 'Can't
Stand It' by David Hine,
performed by Steel Pulse;
'Tu y yo' by/performed by
Ruben Blades; 'Why Don't
We Try' by Raymond Jones,
Larry DeCarmine, Vincent
Morris, performed by Keith
John; 'Hard to Say' by
Raymond Jones, performed
by Lori Perry, Gerald Alston;
'Party Hearty' by William 'Ju
Ju' House, Kent Wood,
performed by Eu; 'Prove to
Me' by Raymond Jones,

Also Published

BFI Modern Classics combine careful research with high-quality writing about contemporary cinema.

If you would like to receive further information about future **BFI Modern Classics** or about other books from BFI Publishing, please fill in your name and address and return this card to us:*
(No stamp required if posted in the UK, Channel Islands, or Isle of Man.)

NAME

ADDRESS

POSTCODE

WHICH **BFI MODERN CLASSIC** DID YOU BUY?

* In North America, please return your card to: Indiana University Press, 601 N. Morton Street, Bloomington, IN 47404, USA

BFI Publishing
21 Stephen Street
FREEPOST 7
LONDON
W1E 4AN